Tove Knight

INVESTOR'S GUIDE

Selecting Shares that Perform

Ten Ways to beat the index

RICHARD KOCH

D0317097

FT
PITMAN
PUBLISHING

London · Hong Kong · Johannesburg · Melbourne · Singapore · Washington DC

PITMAN PUBLISHING
128 Long Acre, London WC2E 9AN
Tel: +44 (0)171 447 2000
Fax: +44 (0)171 240 5771

A Division of Pearson Professional Limited

First published in Great Britain in 1994
This edition published in 1997

ISBN 0 273 62687 6

British Library Cataloguing in Publication Data
A CIP catalogue record for this book can be obtained from the British Library

10 9 8 7 6 5 4 3 2 1

Typeset by Northern Phototypesetting Co. Ltd, Bolton
Printed and bound in Great Britain by Bell and Bain Ltd, Glasgow

The Publishers' policy is to use paper manufactured from sustainable forests.

Contents

This book is dedicated to Lee

Foreword

WHY YOU NEED THIS BOOK

If you are an individual investor, whether you are a stock market novice or a sophisticated player, you will benefit from reading this book. Allow me to lay out five compelling reasons why:

1. *Investment in the stock market leads to a greater compounding of wealth than any other reasonably safe method.*

2. *It is possible to select shares that perform: that beat the stock market average performance.* Many people do, consistently, because they follow a proven approach that fits their personality.

3. *You can too, by selecting one of the ten ways outlined in this book.*

4. *There is no one right way to select shares that perform.* Certain approaches are better than others, but a number of ways, consistently followed, will work. What is important is to select the way that is right for you as an individual, which may be entirely different from what would work for your neighbour, partner or workmate.

> Intrigued? You should be, unless you are a Trappist monk, have no possessions, believe in gut-feel gambling, or are already a multi-millionaire.

5. *This book tells you which approach is right for you as an individual and lays down clearly and simply how to follow it.*

Intrigued? You should be, unless you are a Trappist monk, have no possessions, believe in gut-feel gambling, or are already a multi-millionaire. If none of these disqualifications apply, read on. First, let me explain why no one has yet written a book like this.

WHY THIS BOOK IS A FIRST

There are many books on the stock market but they are all oriented towards the ideas of a particular author or school of thought, not towards the reader and his or her characteristics. This is the first book which stands this approach on its head and is 'market driven' rather than 'production driven': in other words, it describes a number of possible approaches and then helps you to select the one which most fits your personality and expertise.

Are you an extrovert or an introvert? Are you a gambler or a risk-avoider? Can you stick to a consistent, long-term plan, or are you essentially opportunistic? Are you creative or a plodder? Do you prefer to play with numbers or with ideas? Are you a non-conformist or do you feel happier in a crowd? Are you long on courage? Do you search for great leaps forwards or do you think of life as a series of small steps to be taken incrementally? Are you patient or impulsive? All of these attributes should affect your choice of investment approach, so that you get the one that will work for you.

> As with most other things in life, you should not select an approach to investment which is dictated by others and which does not take full account of your own strengths, weaknesses and quirks of personality.

The book is written for the private investor and for those considering investment. We highlight ten possible approaches, all of which have performed well historically. But the approaches differ quite markedly in terms of the knowledge and skill required, and in terms of the personalities to which they are best suited. As with most other things in life, you should not select an approach to investment which is dictated by others and which does not take full account of your own strengths, weaknesses and quirks of personality. There are approaches here which can be used by novices, as well as others that require a great deal of market or quantitative knowledge.

THERE IS NO ONE 'CORRECT' INVESTMENT APPROACH

The joy of private investment is that the approach can reflect your own personality and skills. The investment approach should also vary according to:

- your timescale for investment;
- your personal financial standing and objectives;
- your risk profile;
- the time that you can, and want to, spend on your investing;
- the range of contacts that you have.

AVOID BEING MESMERISED BY GURUS

There *are* certain general rules that apply to all investment activity and which will improve the odds for everyone, and these are covered in Chapter 4. These are the precepts that are common to nearly all successful investors, and this is one of the most valuable chapters in the book. But there are two dangers in following any particular guru, just because he (or she) is an authority or a successful investor.

One danger is that you will get confused when you read the views of a new guru who has equally good credentials as the one you are following. Many books on investment flatly contradict each other. In fact, it's worse than this: many well-known investors are actually inconsistent in their approach, and even give contradictory advice themselves. By trying to put too many strands of thought together, they become confusing, as well as giving you the suspicion that their rules are actually post-event rationalisations attempting to clothe lucky breaks in theoretical precepts. For example, Warren Buffett is rightly one of the most celebrated and successful investors alive, having accumulated eight billion dollars from his successful investments over several decades. But attempts to describe his approach always fall down because he really has at least three or four different methods, and he alternates between them without any evident rationale. This book avoids the danger of confusion by taking ten relatively 'pure' approaches which can be easily understood and followed.

> One danger is that you will get confused when you read the views of a new guru who has equally good credentials as the one you are following.

AVOID WEARING OTHER PEOPLE'S SHOES

The other danger is that you may follow an investment approach that
works very well for Mr X, but which could never work for you, because
you have a different personality, different knowledge or different skills.
For someone without Warren Buffett's extensive personal contacts in
American industry, to attempt to emulate his approach is fatuous, just as
it would be foolish to go in for Value Investing, which requires a high level
of quantitative and accounting skill, if you do not like numbers much. On
the other hand, there are some remarkably successful investors who
would fail an accounting examination. They have certain other attributes
which may or may not apply to you.

A BRIEF GUIDE TO THE TEN WAYS

Way I is called *Follow the Rainmakers*, and suggests shadowing the moves
made by particular successful investors. This Way requires care and
consistency but no particular skill, and can be followed by any investor.

Way II comprises a System for *Backing winners* which is relatively simple,
though it does require daily share price monitoring.

Way III comprises ten different types of *Specialisation*, building on
particular skills that you may have.

Way IV is *Detecting earnings acceleration*, and shows how to invest in
growth companies that are likely to increase their share prices quickly,
sometimes after the growth is already evident. This is higher risk than the
previous three Ways and also requires some basic accounting skills and
reasonable numeracy.

Way V is for extrovert enthusiasts who have time to gather information on
target companies from the outside, and hence is called *Outsider
information*.

Way VI is a guide to *Good business*. Following this Way requires an
analytical cast of mind and a long time horizon, but can lead to attractive
results without taking too many risks.

So can *Way VII*, *Value investing*, which gives accounting rules for buying
low and selling high. Value investing is for the serious, long-term investor.

These seven Ways can be a total approach for all your investments, whereas the last three Ways are all relatively high risk and should only be used for part of a portfolio. *Way VIII* is simple to follow and involves investing in fast growth Third World countries, the so-called *Emerging markets*. This has produced very high returns in the past decade.

The last two Ways are both high risk and complex, but potentially highly rewarding. They both focus on particular types of investments which are quoted on the Stock Exchange but are not normal shares. *Way IX* introduces the capital shares of Split Level Investment Trusts, and hence is called *Opening the SLITs*. *Way X* is concerned with *Warrants*. The book will enable you to find one investment approach that you particularly like and should be able to enjoy operating.

UPCOMING DELIGHTS

The first section of this book explains why it can be fun and profitable to try to beat the stock market, as well as helping you understand the type of investment approach suited to your personality. The second section lists the 'Ten Best Ways' to outperformance, as well as stressing the skills and personality required for each approach to work for you. In general, the 'easier', less time-consuming and less quantitative methods are listed first, and the more recondite and technical ways towards the end of the list.

> The book will enable you to find one investment approach that you particularly like and should be able to enjoy operating.

You should be able to find an approach suited to you. You can take insights from two or three approaches to make your own blend of investment success, but unless there are particularly good reasons to 'mix and match', you are best advised to stick pretty much to one strategy. Having finished the book, you may then understand why some of your investments and approaches have been more successful than others.

Foreword to second edition

The success of the first edition has presented both the opportunity, and the temptation, to update the original material. It is an opportunity because time marches on, insights become more finely honed, and one can adapt observations to recent market developments.

It is a temptation, however, because one is tempted to rewrite history and use the benefit of hindsight to seem more omniscient than one really was.

I have decided to play fair with the reader. I have left the original text exactly as it was, so you can see where I was right and where I was wrong. But I have added updating remarks (see the sections 'An update') so you can also benefit from experience since I wrote. I have also corrected errors, added some new material, and updated graphs where this is necessary to make the point.

The response to the original edition has been extremely gratifying. I hope that my luck holds (and yours too, which is even more important!) with this edition. Happy reading and profitable investing!

Acknowledgements

I have been greatly helped in researching and checking the examples in this book by Joe Cronly and Andrew Laws, both of whom have brought an enormous amount of energy and quantitative rigour to the task.

This book also benefitted greatly from the comments made by the following friends, who all reviewed the first draft of the book: Chris Brace, Robin Field, Bryan Mayson, James Morton, David Norton, Anthony Rice and Clive Richardson.

I am extremely grateful to Professor Harold ('Hal') Leavitt for permission to raid and perhaps distort his extremely original and useful typology of people into Types 1, 2 and 3 (see pages 69–71). The insight is his, though any mistakes made are mine. May I refer those who would like to read a fuller and more accurate account of his views to his new book *Corporate Pathfinders*, published by Penguin, which is highly readable and full of wisdom.

I would also like to thank my friends at Pitman Publishing who have supplied encouragement and criticism in the right proportions, especially Mark Allin, David Crosby, Trish Denoon, Sally Green, Helen Pilgrim, Kate Salkilld and Richard Stagg.

Finally, I am grateful for the help in producing the final printed version of the book, including production of the graphs and tables, given by Marian Clarke and her troupe of supporters.

PART ONE

Strategy for the individual investor

> The intelligent private investor need feel no sense of inferiority in going to battle against the big institutions. There are good reasons why you should be able to do better.

1

Why the stock market?

ARE YOU IN FAVOUR OF MORE MONEY?

Anyone who has any money to save and invest should put a large part of it into the stock market. The reason is boringly simple: the stock market generally does much better than any other reasonable safe investment such as putting the money in a bank or building society. If you had invested £100 in a building society in 1950, it would have matured by 1992 into £813. The same £100 invested in the stock market would have returned £14,198: over 17 times as much!

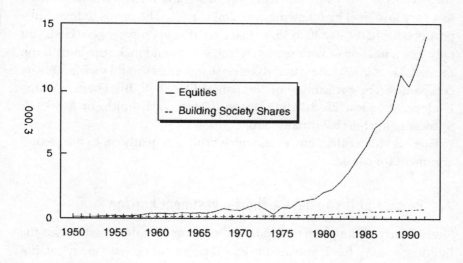

Figure 1.1 **Comparison of equities and building society shares: £100 invested in 1950, net income reinvested**
Source: The BZW Equity and Gilt Study, 1993

Of course, it's not quite as simple as this. If it were, nobody in their right mind would ever put money on deposit with a bank or building society. There are four reasons why stock market investment may not be appropriate for you.

FOUR REASONS FOR CAUTION

1. There is definitely more risk with the stock market

If you put your money in a bank or building society, you generally know exactly what interest you will earn, and you can be almost certain that you will not *lose* money. With the stock market, there are no guarantees. As they charmingly say, prices can go down as well as up, and you could lose all your money. You also cannot depend on receiving a certain amount of regular income with ordinary shares, because this may change or even disappear.

> As they charmingly say, prices can go down as well as up, and you could lose all your money.

The risks can be exaggerated. When people think about risk on the stock market, they think about spectacular company failures like Polly Peck, where the investors have lost all their money. But such events are very rare for large companies, and the risk can be reduced to a very low level by following two simple rules. The first is to invest in a portfolio of shares, say 10 to 15, so that even if one company goes bust, you only lose a fraction of your money, which you should make up on gains on the rest. The second rule is that risk-averse investors should pick large, safe companies. The probability of companies like Shell, BP, Thames Water, Unilever, London Electricity, Hanson, Glaxo, WH Smith, or Marks & Spencer going bust is virtually zero.

There is still a catch, however, which brings us neatly on to the second argument for caution.

2. Be careful if you have a short investment horizon

Over nearly all long time periods, the stock market does better than the building society. But if you are the proud possessor of 'hot money', so hot that it wants to bound around from one place to another, with an underlying desire to get spent, the stock market is not for you. If you have the money to invest for six months or a year, but then want or need to get it back, the stock market is not for you. It is perfectly possible for the stock market to give you back less than you started with.

If, on the other hand, you want to invest for five years or longer, the chances of the stock market returning you a loss is low. In fact, on past form, the chances of the stock market giving you less back than the building society is almost equally low.

The practical answer is that if you are likely to be an investor for two or more years, you should put a certain amount into the stock market, and the rest in the bank or building society or other investments. There is in fact a whole range of these 'other' investments (excluding the stock market, building societies and banks). A rule of thumb for what proportion of free savings (excluding any investment in a home or other higher priority for you) you might invest in the stock market is shown in Table 1.1.

Table 5.1

Investment horizon	Per cent in stock market
1 year or less	0
1–2 years	25
2–3 years	50
4–5 years	75
Over 5 years	90–100

This is, of course, only a rough guide and no-one should make a decision without taking appropriate advice. The more risk averse might want never to put more than half their savings in the stock market, however long their time horizon, while someone with a lot of other assets might decide to put it all in, even if they have a planned use for the money in two years.

3. Do not invest a large lump sum when the stock market is 'high'

The stock market goes in cycles, as shown in a simple way in Figure 1.2.

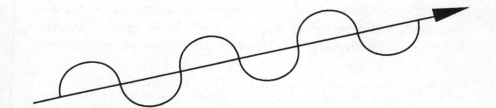

Figure 1.2

The cycles vary in length, as can be seen from the real life chart of the British stock market's performance over a long time (see Figure 1.3). In practice, no one knows when the next cycle will end or what the direction will be over the next few months or years. But if you had invested all your money at the top of the last cycle (in early October 1987), it would have been over five years before you were a very happy investor, whereas if you invested the same lump sum at the bottom of the cycle (in November 1987), you would have felt that you had the Midas touch within a year. A guide as to when the market is high is provided on pages 255–257.

There are two practical conclusions to draw from this. One is that the safest way to invest in the stock market is to put a little in at a time, and continue doing this regularly for years. That way you will get the benefits of the stock market's long-term outperformance without the trauma of trying to pick the right time to get in. (It follows that when you want to realise your money, you should, if possible, get out in the same way, that is, gradually over time.)

The second practical conclusion is that you should be very cautious about investing any money at a time when you suspect that the market is at or near a temporary peak. There are various technical ways of detecting this, though I will only bother you here with two easy ways. The simplest one is not to invest when everybody else is: when it seems that putting money into the stock market is a route to short-term winnings, when new peaks in the stock market are discussed on chat shows and are making headlines in *The Sun* as well as in the *Financial Times*, when it seems you can't lose with the stock market, when the cleaning lady knows all about ICI, that is exactly the time **not** to invest. A crash at such times of limitless confidence is odds on, if only because Fate has a keen sense of humour.

The slightly more technical rule is to look at the 'price earnings ratio' (PE).* When this is more than 17, the stock market is valuing earnings at a historically high level, which can be highly dangerous unless there is good news around the corner. Before the stock market crash of October 1987, the price earnings ratio was 21, which should have indicated danger.

---

*This is the value of the company on the stock market divided by its last year's earnings (profit after tax), and can be easily found by looking at the *Financial Times*. Alternatively, ask someone who knows about the stock market what it is at the moment. Intuitively, it is the number of years that someone is prepared to wait before getting the value of the money the company makes each year (in practice it's much more complicated than this). The higher the number, the higher the value placed on a company or the whole stock market for a given amount of earnings – and therefore the more vulnerable the value is to a shift back to shorter time horizons.

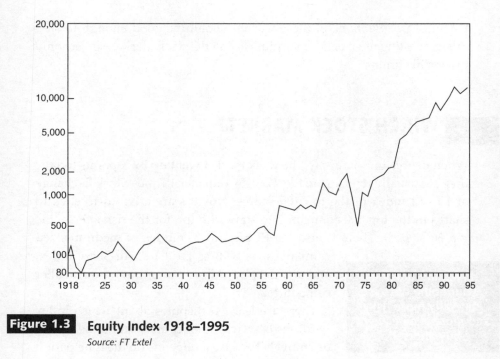

Figure 1.3 **Equity Index 1918–1995**
Source: FT Extel

Similarly, at the time of writing (October 1993) the ratio is 20.1, although the 'prospective' PE based on expected 1993 earnings is lower, at 15.8. Nevertheless, the historic PE is the one you should use (you can't be sure about the future earnings) and at this sort of level caution is required. If the historic ratio is over 17, only invest a small amount until it comes down.

The indicators of possible stock market vulnerability are discussed in more detail in Part Two (pages 255–257).

4. The future is not the past run backwards

Or as the government warning on the ads says, past performance is not necessarily a guide to future performance. This is, of course, true. Fortunately, we ignore most of this nanny-state advice when we lead our normal lives. We do let our experience influence our actions. In life, as at the race track, the form book does have some value. Unless the world changes in a fundamental way (and it may, it may, I'm not against you looking out for such changes), the stock market will out-perform any other normal way of investing your money over the long term.

For most people, none of these reasons should be good enough to stop them investing most of their surplus cash in the stock market, subject only to sensible timing.

WHICH STOCK MARKET?

When people in Britain say 'the stock market went up by X points today', they are usually referring to the 'Footsie' (Financial Times-Stock Exchange or FT-SE) index of the top 100 shares. Novices are advised to stick to shares in the top 100 companies to start with (or, for the risk averse, the top 30 shares). There is also the FT-SE Mid 250 index of medium-sized companies, as well as the FT-A All-Share index, and a variety of indices concentrating on smaller companies.

> **Investing outside your home base is generally more risky and more expensive to buy and sell.**

There are learned disputes about which index performs best, which, of course, cannot be settled definitively because it depends on the time period taken. There is a general tendency for the indices covering all companies or just smaller companies to out-perform the FT-SE 100 index, but the risk is greater. On the whole, though, differences between indices are less important than the differences between shares as a whole on the one hand, and other, inferior savings methods on the other.

There is, of course, no compelling reason to stick to the UK stock market alone. The most popular other market is the US, although leading shares from most substantial markets can be bought through UK stockbrokers, and the *FT* lists daily price changes for these covering 21 foreign stock markets. The attractions of some of these markets are discussed in Part Two, Way VIII. For the time being, however, we will confine ourselves to the UK stock market, with some additional examples drawn from America. Investing outside your home base is generally more risky and more expensive to buy and sell, so unless there is a compelling reason to do otherwise, stick to large UK companies. Their record of success for investors over several generations is excellent.

► **Concluding remarks**

Now you know why to invest in the stock market: the average performance is so good. The next chapter tells you why you can do even better than this.

2

Should you try to out-perform the market?

You could always 'track the market'

The 'do it yourself' way to index track

Which index?

Two ways of making DIY index tracking simpler and cheaper

But is index tracking for wimps?

So seek super-performance, but ...

YOU COULD ALWAYS 'TRACK THE MARKET'

Given the excellent long-term returns from the stock market, you could simply decide that you are **not** going to try to beat the market, simply to equal it. This is a relatively low-risk strategy (provided you do not splurge a large lump sum at the top of the market: see the cautions on pages 7–9 above), and quite easy to arrange.

There are two ways. The easier is to invest your money in a 'Tracker Fund' run by professionals who do this: you can find these funds advertised in the newspapers or ask your financial adviser. There are drawbacks to this method, however, which almost certainly guarantee a slight under-performance against the market index. The Tracker Funds have to pay their operators and will therefore charge a management fee, which covers the administration and marketing costs (your seemingly objective financial adviser may well be receiving a commission; ask him whether he is and how much and require that it is split with you, or better still, find a truly objective adviser who charges on a time basis and rebates you all his commissions).

THE 'DO IT YOURSELF' WAY TO
INDEX TRACK

The slightly more difficult way is to do it yourself. This involves constructing a portfolio which exactly matches the market index you decide to track at the time you decide to get in. You then have to watch for the deletions and additions to the index that take place periodically, and buy and sell accordingly. You can then collect the dividends and either spend the income or reinvest it.

The 'DIY' approach to index tracking is not much practised yet. This is partly due to the effort required, but also because of the high transaction

> It is much more fun, and in the long run probably significantly cheaper, to 'do it yourself'.

costs in buying and selling a large number of small blocks of stock. If you use a normal stockbroker who gives advice and research, he will charge 1.65% commission each time you buy and sell your small portions of stock. The lower cost alternative is to use 'execution only' services which are much cheaper, since for index tracking you don't need advice (in fact, it's positively harmful!). The percentage commission you pay will, however, certainly exceed the real transaction costs incurred by the Tracker Fund (although not necessarily what the Fund charges you!).

Yet do not despair! It is much more fun, and in the long run probably significantly cheaper, to 'do it yourself'. In a moment I will explain two ways round these difficulties. First, though, we must consider which index to track.

WHICH INDEX?

For all but the largest investors, the choice is between the FT 30 or the Footsie 100. The latter may tend to give a slightly better return, although having 100 stocks at any one time is rather burdensome to administer if you are doing it all yourself! If you are, you are probably best advised to stick to the FT 30, which will be relatively low risk and over a long period is very likely to give impressive results. But consider two possible other options …

TWO WAYS OF MAKING DIY INDEX TRACKING SIMPLER AND CHEAPER

One way, which can also make it more fun, is to find a few friends of like mind and start an Index Tracking Club. That way you can share the burden of work involved (for example, one of you doing the buying and selling, one the admin, one keeping an eye on index changes, and so on) and lower your average transaction costs, because you will be dealing in large blocks of stock. You can also take collective pride in working out how much cheaper this option is for you than putting your money into a Tracking Fund.

A second way, although this is not *strictly* index tracking, is to make a random selection from the FT-SE 100 stocks, and have only, say, 20 stocks in your portfolio. You must still be sure to sell any stocks you have that drop out of the index, and to buy a random selection of one fifth of any stocks added. Although you might think that this would not lead to a very close correlation with the total index, financial theory and experiments alike confirm that the benefits of risk reduction by diversification (that is, by buying lots of stocks) fall off rapidly after 15 stocks are acquired. It is likely, then, that your random selection will follow the overall index quite closely, although this cannot be guaranteed. But since there is an equal chance of doing better or worse, the average future 'expected' value of this strategy is the same as buying everything in the index, although with slightly higher risk.

If you adopt a Mini Track Portfolio as suggested above, **you must ensure that it is truly random, and not try to guess which companies are going to do better**. One way to do this is to take the FT-SE in order of market value (listed in the FT and in some Sunday papers), roll a die, take the number indicated as your first stock (if a one, the top stock, if a six, the sixth), and then go down and take every fifth stock. Another way would be to take one from each industry at random, and then put the remaining stocks into a pot and pick out the winners. Or you can work out your own method.

BUT IS INDEX TRACKING FOR WIMPS?

Not necessarily: perhaps a fairer description would be wimps, widows and the risk averse. It is certainly a tame option and not as much fun as those described in the rest of second half of this book. Just to get your greed glands thumping, let's give three examples of above average market performance which could have been predicted (as in fact two of which were, by the author) using the methods described in the rest of this book. It should be stressed that the risks were higher in all cases, but in two cases perhaps not so very high as you might think.

Filofax

This concerns a company most people have heard of: Filofax, which supplies personal organisers. This was a company which was floated on the stock market in April 1987 at 120p and immediately went to 160p and by September 1987 had reached a peak of 207p based on increasing profits and the perception that it was riding the Yuppie boom (see Figure 2.1).

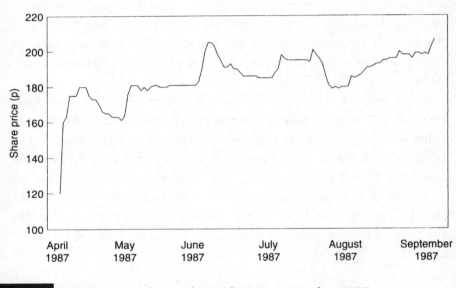

Figure 2.1   **Filofax – initial growth, April 1987–September 1987**
Source: Datastream

None of the principles in this book, however, would have led you to buy Filofax at this time, as it reached an unjustifiably high rating, unsustainable profit margins (at one time reaching over 20% return on sales, which is difficult for any product-based business), and decelerating profit growth. The fall from grace was swift until, by October 1990, the shares had crashed to 13p, signalling that the market thought there was a strong risk of Filofax going bust (see Figure 2.2).

Now comes the time when, as explained in Way IV, (page 139) the brave follower of one of our Ten Ways might have taken a modest interest in Filofax. A financial reconstruction was put together and a different strategy proposed for the company in detail in a public document, which might have persuaded you that, despite all recent appearances, this was a good

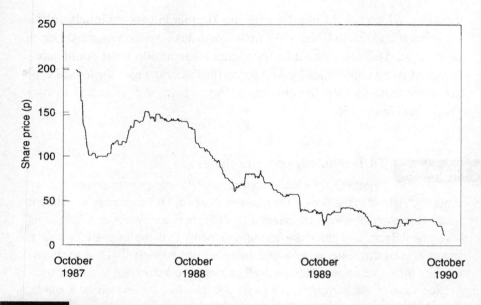

Figure 2.2 **Filofax – share price collapse, October 1987–October 1990**
Source: Datastream

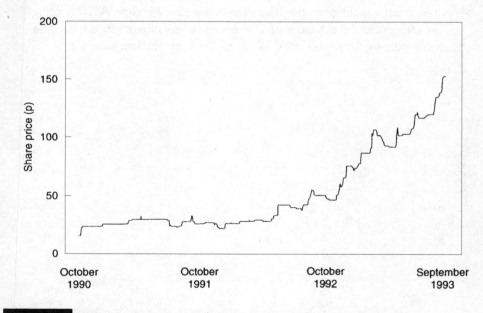

Figure 2.3 **Filofax – Reconstruction, October 1990–September 1993**
Source: Datastream

business, which would not die with the Yuppie. Filofax definitely fulfils the criteria laid out in Chapter VI for a Good Business, so you might have made a modest investment in the rights issue at 30p (you could have obtained some of the stock by contacting the issuers). From the low of 13p, the shares rose to 151p in September 1993, a gain of over 1000% in two years (see Figure 2.3).

✳ EXAMPLE   **TR Technology ordinary shares**

Another example of exceptional performance from one of the Ten Ways highlighted in the book is the ordinary shares of TR Technology investment trust. As explained in Way IX (pages 237–265) these are shares in a Split Level Investment Trust, and there are strong arguments that the ordinary or capital shares in such trusts are undervalued, provided one believes that the trusts can increase their total values at least as well as they have historically. In a rising market such shares will perform much more strongly than the market as a whole, though the reverse is also true. Both these last points can be seen clearly from the graph in Figure 2.4, which shows that the ordinary shares of TR Technology performed badly in the first four months of 1992, falling from around 40p to a low of 18p. At this point the analysis described in Way IX would have clearly signalled that the market and these shares started to climb again. The shares should therefore have been bought when they had risen to the 22–24p range. Anyone doing this (which includes the author) would have made a very nice profit, as the shares reached £1 during September 1993, a rise of 335% in less than six months.

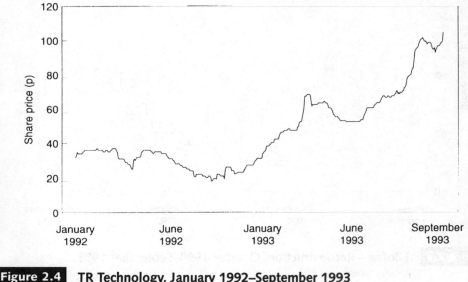

Figure 2.4   **TR Technology, January 1992–September 1993**
Source: Datastream

Airtours shares and warrants

This is cheating a little bit because I never went near Airtours warrants (warrants are a particular type of investment explained in Way X) and only
a small band of warrant enthusiasts were in on this one. Warrants, which are our
tenth way of beating the market and the most speculative, can, at their best,
offer astounding rewards, which in certain circumstances makes it worthwhile to
buy a portfolio of warrants in the hope that one or two of them will make you a
fortune. Such was the case with Airtours warrants in 1991 (see Figure 2.5).*

The shares of this package holiday company are pretty volatile, both because the
market itself goes up and down quickly depending on the weather and the
economy, and because market shares can shift rapidly too. During the early
months of 1991 those in the trade knew that the market was just beginning to
swing up, and that there was more market share available because this upswing

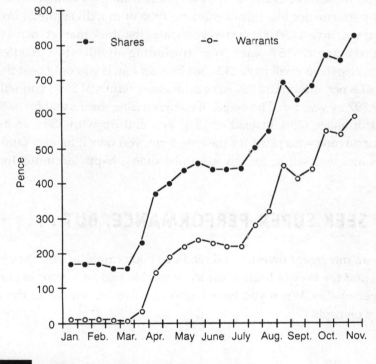

Figure 2.5   **Airtours – Warrants and shares 1991**

Source: The Investor's Guide to Warrants, Andrew McHattie, Financial Times

*I am indebted for this and other examples on warrants to Andrew McHattie, whose excellent book *The
Investor's Guide to Warrants* (in the same series as this book) is the standard reference work on this exciting sector.

had come too late to save ILG Intasun, a big competitor. Therefore, anyone following our advice in Way VI and an expert in the package holiday business (perhaps a manager in it) might have bought the shares in January, February or the first half of March, and seen them rise from 170p to 812p by the end of October, a brilliant rise of 378%.

But someone who had taken a lot more risk and bought the Airtours warrants (that is, an option to buy shares in Airtours in the future), which rose from a possible purchase price of 12p to 590p during the same time, would have been over 4,800 per cent up! I can't cope with these percentages, so to speak in real money, £2,000 invested in Airtours warrants would have realised £98,300, which you will agree is not bad.

Of course, these three examples are exceptional, and you cannot expect to see out-performance like this over a long time or in a diversified portfolio. But if you invest £30,000 for ten years, and the stock market increases by an average of 15% each year (including dividends but after transaction costs), you will have £121,366 by year ten. If you only beat the index by 10% per annum (that is, have an average return of 25%) you will have £279,397 by year ten. The magic of compounding means that for 67% better performance (25% instead of 15%) you end up with 130% more money. For anyone who plans for the long term, you owe it to your family, friends and yourself to see if you can become a happy accumulator.

SO SEEK SUPER-PERFORMANCE, BUT . . .

If you are an intelligent investor and read this book carefully, you should be able to find the Way of beating the stock market that suits your expertise and personality. When you have found it, however, remember three cautionary precepts.

1.   If this is a new approach for you, do it crabwise

Don't commit your fortune overnight. Try it out gradually, with small initial investments, or better still try a six-month 'dummy' period making your decisions and tracking results without actually investing. You will soon find out whether the approach works (although you should compare your results to the market index you choose to beat at the beginning, not to your absolute gain or loss). If you find it too dull having a 'dummy' period, start by only investing a fraction of your ultimate intended investment.

> .... For anyone who plans for the long term, you owe it to your family, friends and yourself to see if you can become a happy accumulator. ....

2.   Never commit money you cannot afford to lose

Wait until you are already showing positive returns before investing fully.

3.   If it doesn't work, go back and 'track the index'

Before you start, set yourself a timeframe and write down your resolution to stop the investment approach by such and such a date if you have not out-performed the market over that period. **Then stick to it.** You may enjoy playing the stock market, but if it is costing you serious money (relative to the index), it is too expensive. Take a modest sum and go to the racetrack or the casino instead from time to time, while investing your real money in the stock market index. I cannot stress this too strongly. Some people can beat the index almost every year, but other intelligent folk consistently fail to do so. In this case, the past is the best (although imperfect) guide to the future. If you under-perform, quit while you're behind. Don't let pride prejudice your long-term wealth accumulation, which can build very nicely thank you by following the index.

> ...... Some people can beat the index almost every year, but other intelligent folk consistently fail to do so. ....

3

David versus Goliath

WHAT HOPE FOR THE INDIVIDUAL INVESTOR?

There are thousands of professional fund managers working away (yes, they do really work these days) in the City, and there is another horde of professionals trying to interest them in buying and selling shares (stockbrokers and their analysts), not to mention another group (company managers and their PR, sorry, investor relations, people) who used to pass on valuable information to the institutions before making it fully available to the stock exchange and the Press (and therefore you and me). The rules on this have been tightened recently, but it is inevitable that if fund managers meet with industrial managers they are going to learn something: otherwise they would stop doing so. It is no secret that some of the investment institutions that have the closest relationships with British industry also have the best performance, and I will leave you to judge whether this is due totally to the institutions' sagacity.

> It is no secret that some of the investment institutions that have the closest relationships with British industry also have the best performance.

The professional fund manager has experience, a free flow of information, access to all sorts of data and charts at the push of a button, and can gauge the mood of the market.

So, as a private investor, should you give up in the face of this apparent superiority of the institutions? Of course not.

It is futile to expect a 'level playing field'. On some terrain the institutions will always have the edge. But you should concentrate on ground where the astute private investor can have strong advantages.

EIGHT ADVANTAGES FOR PRIVATE INVESTORS

These are:

1. Possible infrequency of investment and long time horizon.
2. Greater liquidity.
3. Ability to buy 'small' stocks first.
4. Greater focus.
5. Greater exposure to the real world.
6. Avoidance of the lemming mentality.
7. No outside shareholders.
8. It's your money.

1. Long-term investment horizon

Most institutions are addicted to 'churning', which means buying and selling stocks frequently (stockbrokers love churning). They do this to help justify their existence. Many funds would perform far better if they churned far less often.

Churning sometimes has a role, to cull loss makers, but for good investments it is contrary to common sense. Unless the manager believes that he can judge market timing, and buy back later at a cheaper price, why sell?

2. Greater liquidity

Similarly, if you are a big institution with large holdings in a company, it can be difficult to dispose of them. You might need to hang on to them longer than you really want, in order to avoid driving the price down. If other institutions see that you want to sell, they will know that this 'over-hang' will weaken the shares, so they will not buy, and a vicious circle can be created. To counter this difficulty, large institutions will sometimes 'place' such a holding with a stockbroker at a significant discount to the market price. The stockbroker parcels the shares up into smaller bundles for a number of institutions, takes a small turn, and the shares go up again. Events like this are often reported on the back page of the markets section of the *Financial Times*. Admittedly, the net effect for all institutions is zero, since the bigger institutions lose and the smaller ones (or other big

ones) gain. The real inconvenience for the institutions is not always being able to deal when they
want to without moving the price against themselves.

As a private investor, dealing in relatively
smaller amounts, you can usually buy and sell
your shares when you want to, without paying
over the odds.

> .... Smart private
> investors keep an eye
> on shares and
> instruments that are
> appreciating in value
> quickly and soon will
> be attractive to
> institutions. ....

3. Ability to buy 'small' stocks first

By 'small' I mean low market capitalisation stocks, that is, where the total
quoted value of the company is low. These are generally small companies
plus some instruments (such as warrants) where, although the value of
the *company* is high, the value of the specific class of instrument is not.

This advantage is very important. It means that you can get in on the
ground floor of a high-growth company, which is plainly doing well,
before the institutions can. You still need to check out that it is the reality
and not the hype that is impressive, but you get first turn.

The good news does not stop there. Smart private investors keep an eye
on shares and instruments that are appreciating in value quickly and soon
will be attractive to institutions. Some of these have a rule that they are
not allowed to buy until the market capitalisation reaches £25m or some
other arbitrary number. When it does, there is often a surge in the share
price as institutions move in. Even if they only buy relatively modest
amounts, there is a new factor in the supply/demand equation which can
only be reflected in price. Then other institutions with slightly higher limits take an interest, and so on. Eventually, the share will be incorporated in
the All Share Index, which may cause another round of buying from
'index trackers'. Until this happens the shares may be significantly undervalued.

4. Greater focus

Another huge potential fillip for you is that you can afford to focus your
investments much more than the average fund manager, and concentrate
on those type of stocks where you really do have an advantage in terms of
experience, personality or skills. Fund managers cannot. They have to
make lots of investments and, unless they are quite exceptional individu-

als, they will only be really good at a subset (perhaps a small subset) of these. Funds are generally arranged to cover all industry sectors, so that at any one time the fund will have a presence in all sectors. You can be much more selective, just focusing on one sector or one type of share. This is a crucial advantage for you.

5. Greater exposure to the real world

If fund managers spend most of their working lives actually in the City - and most of them do - they cannot be spending much time observing what is happening in the wealth-creating circles of industry, commerce and leisure. The City is not just a geographical expression: it is a whole world of its own, with a strong culture, closely knit (or in-bred) relationships, and a deeply introverted character. Of course this is, in itself, a 'real world', just the same as universities are 'real worlds': it is just different from most people's world. Industrialists, who depend on the City for capital, often complain that the chaps in the City just don't understand business.

You can turn this to your advantage. Whatever you spend your time doing, be it working in a particular industry or even engaging in a particular leisure pursuit, you can be observing the fortunes of particular companies. You can get to know clues about whether they are doing well or badly, not in terms of financial results, but in terms of what will lead, sooner or later, to those financial results. For example, if it is a consumer product, you can go into the shops where it is sold and see whether its shelf space is increasing or decreasing. Has a new competitor popped up? Or if you know something about what is happening in particular companies, is morale high, or are top management at loggerheads? And so on … it will depend entirely on what you choose to keep an eye on.

In this way you will find out things that are likely to determine the medium-term value of the company, and you will find them out long before those fund managers trapped in the City.

6. Avoidance of the lemming mentality

Another by-product of the City's cultural homogeneity is the tendency for opinions - on the direction of the market, or the prospects for an industry or a company - to coincide. The City is very efficient in generating consensus. Most of the time it may be right, but sometimes it is clearly wrong.

When it is wrong about a particular company, the City professionals (particularly the analysts who forecast earnings) feel let down. They often punish the company by depressing its shares to quite unreasonable levels. This punishment is even more extreme where the management of a company has raised new equity through a rights issue and then failed to deliver the expected short-term profits.

Two recent examples of this are British Aerospace and Hillsdown Holdings. Both raised money through rights issues and issued disappointing results afterwards. Both were then viciously sold by the City, to the point where the market valuation only made sense if there was a serious risk of the companies going bust. Yet the balance sheets of both companies were viable, and there was little such risk.

The dramatic recovery of British Aerospace, as illustrated in Figure 3.1, saw a tripling of the shares during 1992-93, indicating clearly that the stock market had over-reacted to the bad news.

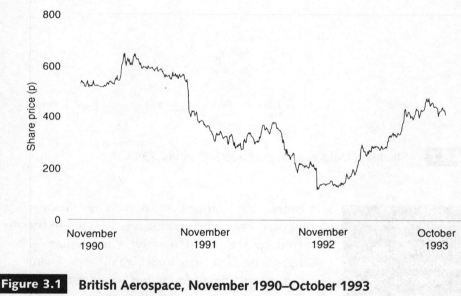

Figure 3.1 **British Aerospace, November 1990–October 1993**
Source: Datastream

Similarly, Hillsdown Holdings, a company that was never in any danger of going bust, and which was consistently profitable and high yielding, saw its shares marked down to an absurd degree during 1992. Someone who bought the shares just after they had started to recover (in the 80p range) would have doubled their money in less than a year, having borne very little risk and received at least one attractive dividend in the period (see Figure 3.2).

British Aerospace and Hillsdown Holdings both illustrate how the lemming mentality of the City leads to over-reaction. The private investor need not share this conventional wisdom (or delusion), and can sometimes obtain real bargains (although one should always wait until the price has bottomed out and started to rise again).

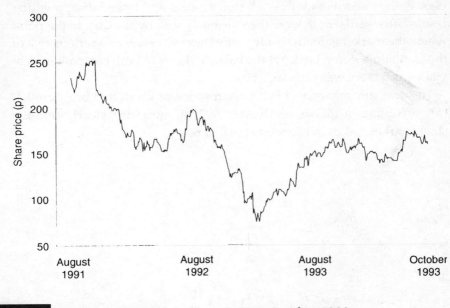

Figure 3.2   **Hillsdown Holdings, August 1991–October 1993**

Source: Datastream

> **Most professionals will only buy once other professionals have already started to do so.**

Of course, conventional wisdom is not always wrong, and even when wrong it is wise not to try to stand up against it too early. When a share is falling, it is best left alone until the fall stops. There is always a problem identifying whether the fall has been overdone, or whether there is some intrinsic reason, which has not yet emerged publicly, that will make the shares continue to fall. In the autumn of 1993, for example, Micro Focus fell alarmingly and continued to do so despite there being no apparent bad news. The firm then issued a profits warning.

The potential advantage for you is that when the price does stabilise and start to creep up, the individual investor can buy without being handicapped by the conventional professional view that this is a share to avoid. Most professionals will only buy once other professionals have already started to do so.

What is true for individual companies is true for the market as a whole. Decade after decade, the persistence of bull markets long after the fundamentals could support them, and then the sudden, extreme corrections, can be explained not by faulty slide rules or computers but by the collective, consensual psychology of the City and other financial markets. Keynes rather kindly called this 'animal spirits'; I call it the lemming mentality.

You need not fall prey to the lemming mentality. The further away you are from the City, the better. And when you notice that it is happening, **and** you really understand the companies whose shares you are buying and selling, you can benefit in ways that are quite beyond the City professionals.

7. No outside shareholders

You don't have to waste time reporting to anyone, and you don't have to do things you think are not right because of company policy, weightings, the need for half yearly profits, or any of the paraphernalia of the modern investment institution. Of course, you should set goals and monitor performance. I will stress below (see pages 47–57) the importance of simple record-keeping. You should certainly not fool yourself. But you don't have to worry about doing anything other than what you genuinely consider to be right.

8. It's your money

A final very obvious but very important point is that you will be viscerally interested in the results, because it's your money. However competent and conscientious, it is impossible to expect professional managers to have the same commitment as owners.

➤ Concluding remarks

The professional fund manager clearly has a valuable role in helping those who cannot manage their own money to channel it into the stock market. But surveys show time and time again that the average performance of fund managers is inferior to that of the market. This is partly due to technical reasons (especially the fact that under-performing shares are periodically made to drop out of the Index), but the important lesson is that fund managers are expensive and generally achieve mediocre results. Individuals can be much more selective, much more aggressive, much more intelligent, much lower cost and much more successful.

The intelligent private investor need, therefore, feel no sense of inferiority in going to battle against the big institutions. There are good reasons why you should be able to do better.

4

Rules to stop you losing

Negative before positive

Concluding remarks

NEGATIVE BEFORE POSITIVE

It might seem odd to tell you what **not** to do before telling you what to do, but there is a good reason. There are multiple routes to success, as outlined in Part Two, and any one of them can work if it suits you. The road to hell, in contrast, is well sign-posted and well travelled. The ways to win are many and unpredictable, but the ways to lose are fewer and entirely predictable. Whichever ladder to winning you climb, you will need to steer clear of the same snakes.

1. Never invest funds you don't own

Even if you are able to, do not borrow money to make equity investments. However high your net worth, this is a fundamentally unsound principle. It has ruined many millionaires and billionaires. Don't let it ruin you. The only thing to invest with is money that you own which is not needed for any other purpose. There must be absolutely no exceptions to this rule.

2. Choose short-term investments with great caution

If you are investing for a relatively short period – by which I mean two years or less – the reason you have this time horizon is because you then want to use the money for something else: school fees, going round the world, a house deposit, or whatever. It would be highly annoying not to have your starting capital when that time comes.

Although the long-term record of shares is excellent, there is always a risk of a significant fall over a period like two years. There is little protection here in picking the most large, stable and 'safe' share, because if there is a general market decline, then GUS, Marks & Spencer and Grand Metropolitan will fall in line.

There are some suitable investments for the short term, but they are 'bonds' (that is, interest bearing securities that are traded) rather than 'equities'. One of the best of these is index linked gilts, which generally increase in value steadily over time, although even here there could be a drop of, say, 10%. But you are less likely to beat the building society by very much.

On the whole the stock market is not a good medium for short-term, 'hot' money.

3. Do not overdiversify your portfolio

In other words, never hold too many stocks. Warren Buffett called over-diversification the Noah's Ark technique: 'one buys two of everything and in the end owns a zoo'.

Why? There is a purely negative reason, in that holding more than about 15 stocks does little to decrease risk, so, given the time and expense involved, why bother? But the positive reason is much more powerful. If you possibly can, you should know the companies you invest in extraordinarily well. This is very difficult if you invest in a large number of companies. It is better to know a few things rather well, or one thing very well, than it is to know something about a lot of things.

> On the whole the stock market is not a good medium for short-term, 'hot' money.

Another positive reason is that with fewer stocks, you will inevitably pause longer, think harder and weigh the buy or sell decision more carefully. You will also be more vigilant in keeping an eye on them and will stand much less chance of missing any necessity to sell, lighten or increase your holding.

But how many is too many? It depends partly, but only partly, on the amount of time you have for your investments. Fingers used in tennis is perhaps the best guide. Most top players use only five, and I think this is a pretty fine number of stocks to hold at any one time. Some (double handed) players use ten, which can also work well. Between five and ten is not a bad policy.

4. Only invest if you are confident

Investing in the stock market is not like picking a winner at Aintree, or even at Epsom, although many (loss making) punters behave as though it is. Before you invest you should be confident about the medium- and long-term prospects for the company. Note that I say the company, not the shares. You should not invest because you consider the shares 'a strong bet'. You must first look at the company and assess, by numbers or otherwise, whether it has a good future of growth ahead of it (one good way to assess this is to look at its past). Then you must consider whether the shares are fairly priced, undervalued or overvalued.

> ...... Tips belong on the racecourse, and even there they are usually wrong. ....

One of the advantages of having a small portfolio of 5–10 stocks is that you will not be tempted to include a few 'speculative long shots'. In my experience, both on the stock market and in venture capital, the 'speculative long shots' nearly always disappoint, and it is the investments originally seen as safe but unexciting that sometimes become the 'stars' giving mega-returns.

5. Never buy on tips

You have probably been approached from time to time by friends or acquaintances offering you 'hot tips' based on rumours, or information close to the 'inside'. Never, ever, buy shares as a result. For one thing, it just may be inside information, in which case you and your informant may be committing a serious criminal offence. But in this case virtue comes cheap, because my advice would be the same even if the use of insider information were made compulsory. It is just not a sensible thing to do. You can't check the veracity or the importance of the data. In some cases, there may be a deliberate attempt to 'ramp' the shares by those who have already bought (and plan to sell soon). In other cases, an honest (but not necessarily competent) person is trying to convince themselves that they made the right decision.

Tips belong on the racecourse, and even there they are usually wrong. Avoid.

6. Do not follow the crowd

Resist the lure of fashion investing: going with the current fad. You will only beat the mass of investors by following a different path. Whichever one of the Ways from Part Two that you select, stick to it for the period you have set and do not be put off by negative comments from analysts about your stocks or be seduced by other approaches or recommendations. You must still convince yourself, of course, that you are right, but unless you have important new information since you made your original decision, do not be moved.

7. Never average down when the price is falling

'Averaging down' means adding to your holding of a stock you already have at a lower price than you previously paid for it, in order to lower the average acquisition price. This is a practice often recommended by stockbrokers (to generate volume and, if they advised the purchase in the first place, to pretend that they are still right), but it is surprisingly prevalent among private investors. Have you never averaged down?

Yet it is an unsound principle. The price at which you first bought a stock is totally irrelevant to whether you should buy or sell now. The only issue is whether, with the information you now have, the company has a good future and the shares are undervalued. Only this should impel you to buy, or indeed to hold, a stock: if you cannot confidently say 'yes' to the two points above, then sell. Neither the company, its customers, its competitors, nor the stock market cares two hoots what price you bought your shares at: it is a matter of total indifference to 99.99 recurring to infinity per cent of the universe. Your original price, compared to the current price, should not lead you to emotional reactions like the roulette player who believes that because he has bet on red for the last ten spins and lost each time, red has a more than equal chance of coming up next. Both reactions are statistically wrong and should be avoided. Remember the old saying that however much a share has fallen, it can fall the same percentage amount again. This is true, until it becomes worthless.

> Remember the old saying that however much a share has fallen, it can fall the same percentage amount again.

There is another, key consideration. I have stressed above that markets often tend to over-react by pushing a share up or down more than is justified when there is some important, surprising news: at least they do, once the momentum gets started (which may be some little time after the news has broken). This might lead you to think that in some circumstances averaging down is perfectly sensible, since your share's price might have been punished more than is due. I will deal with whether this is correct just below the next example. **But even if you are sure the company is good and the shares are seriously undervalued, you should not start buying more until you are sure the fall has stopped.** The stock market can be like a raging torrent, and it is foolish to step in its way. If everyone wants to sell a stock, and no-one wants to buy, the market makers will force the price lower and lower until eventually some substantial buyers emerge. Unless (and this is unlikely) you are a big buyer who can yourself 'call the bottom', it would be foolish for you to buy on the way down. A good rule is to wait until the price has been stable or rising for at least three consecutive trading days, to include at least one day of a price increase.

You buy shares in JollygoodCo at 50p. They soon start to fall.

EXAMPLE ✳

Day 1	50p	
Day 2	52p	
Day 3	49p	
Day 4	46p	
[...]		
Day 15	30p	
Day 16	29p	
Day 17	29p	
Day 18	29p	
Day 19	29p	**STILL WRONG TIME TO BUY (No price rise)**
Day 20	27p	
Day 21	24p	
Day 22	22p	
Day 23	23p	
Day 24	23p	
Day 25	23p	
Day 26	24p	**BUY**

So much for the tactics, but should you make it a rule *never* to average down? Or, given frequent market over-reaction, should you not positively relish it? To help you decide, let me lay out my experience:

- Most people who average down lose money by doing so.
- This is partly, but only partly, because they tend to increase their holding too soon.
- The market often over-reacts to bad and *unexpected* news about a basically sound company.

- But sometimes the market does the opposite: it is right about the trend, but does not yet suspect how bad it is. Some shares start falling and never recover to anywhere close to their original levels.

- In general, it is better to add to holdings which are already showing a profit ('averaging up') than it is to holdings which are already showing a loss.

On balance, my advice is as follows:

- *Only 'average down' with extreme caution, and after much deliberation.*
- *Do not do it more than once a year.*
- *Only do it if you are sure the company's future is good and the shares are undervalued.*
- *Do not allow one stock to take up more than 25% of the value of your portfolio (this is an absolute maximum, not a target).*
- *Never 'average down' more than once for the same stock.*
- *Never 'average down' until the price has already been stable or rising, with at least one day's rise, for the previous three days.*

You might think this advice is so hedged about that you wished I had simply said, 'Never average down'. If the complexity above bothers or perplexes you, simply follow the prohibition! You may miss a chance to make a killing, but you are more likely to avoid large losses. And remember, if you *don't* 'average down', but simply hold your shares, and the medium-term future works out as you expect, you will eventually scrub out your current loss and make a nice profit simply from the shares you now own. Worse things happen than that, and if you are wrong and the company is a lemon, you will have avoided shipping more good money after bad.

8. Never be afraid to sell at a loss

This is the other side of the 'averaging down' coin. Some astute observers believe that you should **always** cull your loss makers once they have fallen a pre-determined amount (the range of 7–10% is most popular). This is part of the basis for the second of our Ways to beat the market in Part Two of the book.

If a share has fallen relative to the market as a whole (an important qualification), the onus is on you to say why you should keep it. You must have a good reason for doing so.

9. Learn from your experience

Your personal experience of investment, if analysed carefully, will probably show recurrent patterns of behaviour. If you divide your historic portfolio – that is, all the shares you have ever owned – into three categories, organised by the success or otherwise of the investments, it's likely that you will gain a lot of insight by asking what is common about all or some of the investments in each category.

> Categorise your investments as Winners, Losers, and Average

What I am driving at is for you to categorise your investments as Winners, Losers, and Average (in all cases relative to the market), then to look at the Winners and find a few common themes about them, either in terms of the types of company, how closely you know them, why you bought them, or any other common factors. Then repeat the process for the other two categories.

It may be that you have a computer-like memory and can do this categorisation off the top of your head. Or perhaps you have just been investing for a year, you bought nine stocks, and three have scored way above the market, three way below, and the other three in the middle. But the chances are that you might think it a daunting experience to so categorise your investments. You have my sympathies, for I have been there – I know how difficult it can get to keep track of the length of time held, the real profit after transactions costs, the compound annual return for a gain of 17.8% held over eight months and four days, the lack of records of what the stock market index did over that period, and so on.

Fear not, relief is at hand! The next chapter will provide an approach to record-keeping for your portfolio which is original, simple and also quite exciting! Its major benefit is that a series of these records will show quickly and painlessly your real winners and losers.

For the time being I am going to assume that you know what these are. Now conduct your analysis of the similarities in each of categories: Good, Bad and Indifferent. Your insights should be fascinating: obvious in retrospect, but perhaps containing lessons that should lead to important changes in your behaviour! For example, my own post-experience analysis led to the following conclusions:

(a) The **Winners** were mainly:
- companies I knew personally;
- in industries I understood;

- run by people whom I knew.

(b) The **Losers** were:
- penny stocks; *or*
- technology shares (I do not understand technology); *or*
- tips from friends.

It was not until I did this exercise that I decided never to buy any of the above again (except technology unit trusts, where I would not have to pick the individual shares). My portfolio's performance has improved greatly since!

10. Beware of penny shares

Penny shares have inflated and these days are those under 30p (some even say under £1). There were some fantastic apparent gains from penny shares in the 1980s, but I have seen no statistical evidence that a majority of penny share buyers beat the market except in periods of exceptional hype like the run up to the Crash of 1987. Most penny shares are low quality, illiquid, expensive to buy or sell and highly speculative. Many are in companies run by people of dubious repute. Some just represent the last resting place of once great companies before their formal burial.

If you want controlled fun, with the prospect of real upside, but in quality companies, go for one of our last two Ways to beat the market instead: the ordinary or capital shares of Split Level Investment Trusts (Way IX), or warrants (Way X).

11. Do not invest heavily when everyone else is

As mentioned before, do not commit major funds to the market when it is reasonably *possible* that the market is hitting a cyclical high. One simple way to avoid this is never to invest when the market is within 3% of its all-time high. Another is not to invest when the popular newspapers are stock market crazy.

12. Balance patience and prudence

There are two opposite schools of thought and practice which should be mentioned. One is the 'long-termist' approach which holds that there are almost no circumstances in which you should sell shares in a 'good' company. According to this school, the trick is to find a few such companies over your life as an investor and then just stick with them. The opposite philosophy is that markets are volatile, in the long run we are all dead, and that no one ever went broke by taking a profit.

My view is that it rather depends on how skilled you are likely to be at identifying even a few good companies. Not many people are good at doing this (although in my view, with the right training and encouragement to keep their eyes open, many more could be). As will be stressed in Chapters 6 and 7, and throughout Part Two, a lot depends on your own attributes.

The best general position, though, may be three-quarters towards the 'long-term' view above. There are no general rules, but some guidelines may help:

- *Do not be too patient with your under-performers.*
- *Decide in advance if you have a target selling price above your cost price.*
- *Even if the share reaches the target price, continue to hold (nervously) until the shares run out of steam (see the example below).*
- *If you can afford to, do not set a target price and continue to hold your winners for a very long time.*
- *If your shares double in value in a short time, and you are thinking of selling, only sell half (or if you have to, three-quarters) and lock the rest away.*

✳ EXAMPLE   You buy The Excellent Yo-Yo Company shares at 100p. You set a target price of 150p. The rule proposed is that you continue to hold, even after the target price has been reached, unless either the price breaks down through the target price or the price declines for three consecutive sessions, whichever happens first:

Day 1	100p	
Day 2	105p	
[…]		
Day 89	147p	
Day 90	150p	
Day 91	150p	
Day 92	150p	
Day 93	153p	
Day 94	160p	
Day 95	170p	
[…]		
Day 101	205p	
Day 102	205p	
Day 103	200p	
Day 104	195p	
Day 105	190p	
Day 106	190p	**SELL**

Concluding remarks

Remember that these are all general guidelines to help avoid the unnecessary mistakes made by private investors. More positive and selective options will be given in Part Two. But first, a system of record-keeping that is simple and fun.

5

Record-keeping for fun

Why keep records at all?

Objections to this approach

Software

How about your portfolio?

The chapter title is provocative. Everyone knows that the downside of stock market excitement is the mounting pile of documents that needs filing, the arrival of the contract notes, keeping the certificates safe, not to mention the dreaded tax records. Then even the potentially interesting task of looking at performance often gets bogged down in cross-referencing data, checking dates and cost of acquisition, stock market levels, and trying to work out your compound annual return of Southern Utilities that you bought for 45.7p (after expenses) on January 3 and sold for 54.2p (after expenses) on May 4 the following year. Was this a good deal or not? You may scratch your head for a long time before you decide, and even then you're not sure you have applied the right criteria. (Make up your mind. My answer is given at the end of this chapter.)

> The downside of stock market excitement is the mounting pile of documents.

Then you may do what many private investors do: only revalue your portfolio when the market or your shares have recently had a strong run. When you come back to look at your performance, the data points are oddly spaced out in time. There is a limit to what you can learn from such data, not to mention the failure to take decisions in the interim, often at the time you need them most.

There is a simpler and better way. But first let us consider ...

WHY KEEP RECORDS AT ALL?

There are only two reasons: (1) for tax (capital gains tax (CGT), and income tax on dividends) purposes; and (2) feedback: to help you see how you are doing, and improve your performance accordingly (and sometimes facilitate a spot of quiet gloating!).

The first insight is that these are actually two quite different purposes and require quite different records. Everything to do with tax is inherently boring to anyone except a tax expert, and like anything else tinged with handing over money to a wasteful bureaucracy, is depressing too. So let's dispose of that side of things as quickly as possible.

1. The tax records

Ideally, you should have this handled for you by your accountant (or, in the rare case that you have a good bank, by them), who should be sent or copied all data and left to get on with it. Your volume of dealings may not justify such expense, however, and in any case, the more you can do yourself, the lower the professional cost, so this is how to 'do it yourself'.

First, file your contract notes of purchases and sales in a ring binder in order of date, that is, with the most recent on top. Adding a new note is thus relatively easy, and you can always find what you want. Stick to this procedure even if you have more than one stockbroker: date, not broker, is what is important. This is all you will need for capital gains tax purposes. (There is no need to keep any statements from your broker once you have settled up.)

Second, when you have received dividends, record the date, company, amount received (the cheque to you), and the tax credit. Then file the tax credit, again in date order.

That is it. You will need to look at the records and conduct some *ad hoc* analysis to see that you are using up your capital gains tax allowance, or to calculate your CGT liability and how to reduce or eliminate it, prior to April 6 each year. And you will also need to report your dividends received and tax credits on your income tax return. Otherwise, these records can be left in their drawers.

No, that was not very exciting. But here come ...

2. The fun records

You will first need to fill in a working sheet like the one shown in Table 5.1. At the top fill in the date. You will have to decide how often to make this analysis: I suggest once a quarter, preferably at the start of January, April, etc. Then, record the level of the FT index which you have decided is most relevant for you (probably the FT-SE 100), and, once you are doing this for the second quarter, the percentage change in the index since the last time. Then simply list in any order you like, all the shares you currently own, and record for each the current middle market price (the one in the papers), the number of shares you own (look on the contract note or the certificate if you can't remember!), and then multiply these together to arrive at the value. Now you will want to compare this to the value the last time you did the analysis, as you have already done for the FT-SE 100 index.

Table 5.1

Working sheet number: 2

Date:		FT-SE 100:	2803.7	Change:	+2.9%
Share	Price (pence)	Number	Value now £	Last value £	Change %
Embassy	100	8,000	8,000	7,345	+8.9
GWR Holdings	730	2,000	14,600	13,600	+7.4
Southern Utilities*	46	15,000	6,900	6,700	0.0*
Executive Yo-Yo	117	15,000	17,550	15,150	+15.8
Tea Time Radio	10	50,000	5,000	7,500	-33.3
Engulf & Devour	320	5,000	16,000	13,500	+18.5
United Waxworks	33	60,000	19,800	14,400	+37.5
Total			87,850	78,395	+12.1%

* new purchase

There are already many interesting things on this working sheet, but to make it fully useful, transpose the data on to the Portfolio Performance Sheet (Table 5.2), but ranking the shares in descending order of performance (measured by percent change), as over:

Table 5.2

Portfolio performance sheet number: 2				
Date:		FT-SE 100:	2803.7	Change: +2.9%
Rank	Share	Value now £	Last value £	Change %
1	United Waxworks	19,800	14,400	+37.5
2	Engulf & Devour	16,000	13,500	+18.5
3	Executive Yo-Yo	17,550	15,150	+15.8
4	Embassy	8,000	7,345	+8.9
5	GWR Holdings	14,600	13,600	+7.4
6	Southern Utilities*	6,900	6,900	0.0*
7	Tea Time Radio	5,000	7,500	-33.3
Total		87,850	78,395	+12.1%

* new purchase

Note that a line is drawn across the page (preferably in red ink) showing those shares which performed above the market average of 2.9% and
those which under-performed it (if any share exactly matched the index,
draw two lines either side of the share).

The treatment of additions to and sales from the portfolio needs a brief
discussion, before commenting on the advantages of this approach. The
method which I prefer is to add purchases to the first sheets they can
appear on, and to write in their last value as the actual total purchase cost,
even though this 'last value' did not actually appear on the previous quarter's sheet at all (since the shares were not then purchased). This is a bit
hard on the new share, since it is ranked against shares which have had a
whole quarter and the new share may have been in just a few days and
also because the purchase costs are implicitly against it. However, the fact
that it is a new purchase is indicated with an asterisk, so you can make
whatever allowance you want. Then when you sell the share, the result
should be recorded in the next quarter's sheets with the value taken as the
net sale price realised. This will also 'unfairly' depress the relative performance somewhat, but is necessary for completeness. Any other system I
have tried would mislead you more, but you are welcome, of course, to
improve on this.

The results show very good performance overall, beating the market by 9% in one quarter. The only evident concern is Tea Time Radio. Those who have read the preceding chapter would probably decide to jettison this share before it lost any more.

Note that nowhere on either sheet is the original cost of any of the shares. This is deliberate. Original cost is of no relevance now. Just look at how things are performing now.

Our portfolio holder takes no further buying or selling action for the next three quarters. Her results in the next quarter are shown in Table 5.3.

Table 5.3

Portfolio performance sheet number: 3

Date:		FT-SE 100:	2897.70	Change:	+3.3%
Rank	Share	Value now £	Last value £	Change %	
1	Executive Yo-Yo	19,500	17,550	+11.1	
2	United Waxworks	21,780	19,800	+10.0	
3	Engulf & Devour	17,250	16,000	+7.8	
4	Embassy	8,000	8,000	0.0	
5	Southern Utilities	6,750	6,900	-2.2	
6	GWR Holdings	13,150	14,600	-10.0	
7	Tea Time Radio	3,000	5,000	-40.0	
Total		89,430	87,850	+1.8%	

This is not such a happy picture. The portfolio has gone from well exceeding the market change to under-performing it, and only 3 of the 7 shares did better. Arranging the data in this way should lead to questioning of the under-performing shares, and probably to sale of some. Certainly, Tea Time Radio, which has been bottom twice running and has lost 60% of its value since we started, is long overdue for the chop. But nothing was done, with the following results (see Table 5.4) next time.

Table 5.4

Portfolio performance sheet number: 4

Date:		FT-SE 100:	2812.5	Change:	–2.9%
Rank	Share	Value now £	Last value £	Change %
1	Embassy	9,160	8,000	+14.5
2	United Waxworks	22,870	21,780	+5.0
3	Southern Utilities	7,050	6,750	+4.4
4	GWR Holdings	13,150	13,150	0.0
5	Executive Yo-Yo	18,760	19,500	-3.8
6	Engulf & Devour	16,390	17,250	-5.0
7	Tea Time Radio	1,500	3,000	-50.0
Total		88,870	89,430	-0.6%

Frankly, these results are a bit of a surprise. Nothing we have seen so far would lead us to expect Embassy to have become this quarter's star performer. The main disappointment is the poor performance this time from The Executive Yo-Yo Company, which was a star turn in each of the previous two quarters. Engulf & Devour is moving pretty fast down the list, as sentiment turns against conglomerates and as rumours emerge that its last bite is proving indigestible. Still, some things are predictable. United Waxworks remains in the top two, and Tea Time Radio remains well last.

So, on to our final quarter's results (see Table 5.5).

Southern Utilities maintained its good recent run, and was sold at a good profit. Executive Yo-Yo rebounded nicely. United Waxworks fell out of the top two, but it would be churlish to call a 13.9% quarterly rise anything other than good. GWR and Embassy did okay, as is their general wont. Engulf & Devour continued to slip. Not perhaps a surprise, but a nasty dent on the total result, was the suspected final demise of Tea Time Radio, suspended at a half penny.

If we were to look at these results over the full year, some imputations can be made:

- *The portfolio contains two apparent stars: United Waxworks (ranks 1, 2, 2, 3), The Executive Yo-Yo Company (3, 2, 5, 2). These showed increases of 71.9%*

and 41.6% respectively over the period 1 valuation, and if the portfolio had not had and kept these over the period, it would have been unimpressive or in deep trouble.

- *Embassy is an erratic but, over time, reasonable performer (4, 4, 1, 5).* It beat the market in three out of four quarters and only under-performed slightly in that one.
- *GWR (5, 6, 4, 4) is going nowhere.*
- *Engulf & Devour (2, 3, 6, 6) started well, but then faded badly.* The warning signals already there by period 4, and it should have been sold then. Certainly it should be sold now, unless the portfolio owner knows something few other people do (it is always possible she does).

Table 5.5

Portfolio performance sheet number: 4

Date:		FT-SE 100:	2870.9	Change:	–2.1%
Rank	*Share*	*Value now £*		*Last value £*	*Change %*
1	Southern Utilities*	8,130*		7,050	+15.3
2	Executive Yo-Yo	21,450		18,760	+14.3
3	United Waxwork	26,050		22,870	+13. 9
4	GWR Holdings	13,930		13,140	+6.0
5	Embassy	9,435		9,160	+3.0
6	Engulf & Devour	15,275		16,390	-6.8
7	Tea Time Radio	0**		1,500	-100.0
Total		*94,270*		*88,870*	*+6.1%*

* At time of sale during quarter
** Shares suspended, assumed worthless

Tea Time Radio (7, 7, 7, 7) was consistently awful. If this had been sold, as it clearly should have been, after period 2, £5,000 would have been saved and overall portfolio performance boosted considerably.

OBJECTIONS TO THIS APPROACH

The thoughtful reader might object, 'but doesn't that imply constant extrapolation of trends ... what happens when trends reverse?' This is an excellent question. The point is, with this sort of analysis you can take action when that happens.

Another objection is, 'What if I know that the company is really going to grow its earnings over the medium to long term? I don't buy shares to speculate with short-term decisions, but to lock away for the long term.' My answer is, 'Fine, as long as you are right. But you might still want to do this sort of analysis, perhaps on a half-yearly or annual basis, just so you appreciate how much inaction in the short and medium terms can cost you, even if you are totally right.'

This type of analysis fits happily alongside any of the Ten Ways to beat the stock market, and is strongly recommended whichever Way you select.

SOFTWARE

There are several software packages for personal computers now available that, for the technologically inclined, make record-keeping and analysis even more fun.

Typical features include:

- automatic updating of share prices
- valuations of the total portfolio
- graphing of share prices and portfolio valuations
- adjustments for changes to the number of shares, such as scrip issues and rights issues
- capital gains tax calculations.

Prices start at around £50, although you can pay thousands for a very sophisticated package. You can, however, obtain a very good package for a modest cost. Advertisements detailing the features, and reviews of the software, often appear in financial publications, including the *Investors Chronicle*.

HOW ABOUT YOUR PORTFOLIO?

Possibly you are intrigued enough to rush off and rearrange your portfolio analysis to tell you which shares have performed best for you and to yield up similar insights. But first, what was your answer at the beginning of the chapter to the performance of Southern Utilities?

MY VERDICT ON SOUTHERN UTILITIES

The same type of analysis leads me to conclude that it was a potentially good share that was sold too early. Its portfolio performance (6, 5, 3, 1) was initially disappointing but then improved greatly. When it finally sprang to life, the portfolio's owner, nervous at the start, took the opportunity to sell at a reasonable profit. Many people do this sort of thing, but it is usually a mistake. Any share that tops a quarter's list is worth holding on to, at least until it begins to disappoint again.

You will almost certainly not have come to any such conclusion at the start, though I gave you the starting and closing data. That is because it was an unfair question, that neglected to tell you what happened in between, and also what happened to the FT-SE index in between. In my imaginary example, the FT-SE moved sideways in this period (up only 5.5%), so the rise of 18.6% (after expenses) in Southern Utilities still looks good. It is also more than could have been earned in the building society. But the point about the sort of rolling value analysis introduced in this chapter is that point-to-point comparisons against your cost are simply not the right way to look at things. The correct approach is to look at the trend, particularly in the recent past.

Why you need your own approach

Mailing Bibles to Hindus

The value of simplicity

A brief description of the ten Ways

How are investors different?

Concluding remarks

MAILING BIBLES TO HINDUS

Most investment gurus try to convert you to their own approach. It is about as subtle and effective as Victorian attempts to convert Hindus to Christianity by mailing them Bibles.

Successful investment is a very personal business. All successful investors have their favourite techniques, experiences, contacts and expertise. You are unlikely to be able to emulate George Soros, Sir James Goldsmith or Warren Buffett simply by observing what they do, just as you are unlikely to develop into a top flight tennis player simply by gluing yourself to the TV during Wimbledon.

> A great deal of advice from different gurus will be contradictory and leave you wondering which one is right.

In fact, it's even more difficult to learn from investment gurus, because they are often inconsistent – they say several different things in different places, and they sometimes do things that are at odds with their pronouncements.

An even worse fate awaits you if you try to take in messages from more than one investment guru. A great deal of advice from different gurus will be contradictory and leave you wondering which one is right. Fortunately, there is a better way.

THE VALUE OF SIMPLICITY

There is no need for investment philosophies to be complicated. Putting a philosophy into practice may require training, application and experience, but it should be possible to describe the philosophy, the investment approach, in a simple and straightforward way. In fact, simplicity may be *essential* if you are to understand and embrace a particular approach.

For you to be a successful investor requires emotional commitment to your approach as well as intellectual agreement with it. It requires 'visceral understanding': a blend of mind, heart and gut identification. All of the approaches described in Part II are presented in a simple way, and are relatively 'pure' descriptions of a particular approach. The key is to select the approach which is best for you personally.

A BRIEF DESCRIPTION OF THE TEN WAYS

The section below will describe how investors are different and which Way is likely to fit your requirements. The section will refer to the number of each Way, so it is useful to provide a brief summary of what each Way is:

Way	Short name	Likely to be suited to ...
I	Rainmakers	Any investor
II	Backing winners	Any investor able to monitor share prices daily
III	Specialisation	An investor with particular expertise in any area
IV	Earnings acceleration	An investor with some accounting knowledge
V	Outsider information	Risk taking extroverts
VI	Good business	Long-term investors
VII	Value investing	Patient, analytical investors
VIII	Emerging markets	Long-term, risk seeking investors
IX	SLITs	Sophisticated, calculating investors
X	Warrants	Well heeled risk takers

HOW ARE INVESTORS DIFFERENT?

There are seven major differences:

1. Timescale for investment.
2. Personal financial standing and objectives.
3. Risk profile.
4. Time you can spend.

5. Range and type of contacts.
6. Financial and quantitative skills.
7. General personality.

1. Timescale for investment

You are not advised to commit a major part of your funds to the stock market unless you have at least a 2-year horizon. Beyond this, however, there is a range: 5, 10 … 50 years.

For those with a shorter time horizon, the following methods discussed in Part II are suitable: I, II, III, IV, IX and X.

Those with a longer time horizon can pick any approach, but the following Ways are likely to benefit especially from a longer play: V, VI, VII and VIII.

2. Personal financial standing and objectives

If you have fairly limited funds to invest, the following Ways are still suitable: I, II, III, IV, VI, VII. Not suitable, because they are more speculative, are VIII, IX and X.

It is important for everyone to be clear about why they are investing, because this, in itself, may influence the investment approach. I differentiate between the following primary motivations:

(a) *Standard of living motivations.* Here you mainly want extra money in order to raise your future standard of living, making specific purchases, or to reduce or eliminate your borrowings and the worry that goes with them. Unless you are willing to postpone using the money indefinitely, this will imply a short time perspective and the comments in (1) above are relevant.

(b) *Lifestyle motivations.* Here you wish to accumulate wealth in order to be able to make a future radical change in your lifestyle. This could be early retirement, or a change in working hours to enable you to spend more time with your family, or the time to develop new friendships, to take up a time-consuming hobby, to travel round the world, to be free to undertake community or charitable work, or to devote yourself to painting or any other artistic expression. All of these motivations will have timescale implications … and a medium- to short-investment horizon. Again, if it is towards the short term, look at (1) above.

(c) *Buffer/accumulation/legacy motivations.* Some people do not have an instrumental view of investment, that is, they are not principally investing for a particular future event. Rather, they wish to add to their wealth for a variety of other reasons: for added security, in case their income should fall; because they enjoy being rich and would like to be richer, without any propensity to spend the added wealth; or simply to be able to leave a large sum behind to family, friends or charity. All of these are long-term motivations, and such investors can pick any approach, but may wish to benefit from the longer-term approaches mentioned at the end of (1) above.

> ....Whatever the timescale, it is important for you to know why you want to accumulate wealth.......

Whatever the timescale, it is important for you to know why you want to accumulate wealth, at least so that you can enjoy the process as it unrolls.

3. Risk profile

Your willingness to take risks is partly a matter of how much spare cash you have, and of your time horizon, but it is also to some extent independent of mere economic considerations: a matter of how comfortable you are with risk, whether you really hate to lose money, or positively enjoy the thrill of high-risk games. Be careful here. Most people like to think that they are risk takers, but genuine risk takers are pretty rare. If losing money would make you miserable, don't take serious risks, even if you can afford to do so. In particular, if you are risk averse, do not follow Ways VIII, IX or X.

4. Time you can spend

The amount of time you can spend on your investment activities is important in selecting your approach. If you have only a few hours a week (including time spent reviewing the financial press), stick to one of the following Ways: I, VII, VIII. If you have a bit more time but not oodles (say between 5 and 10 hours per week) you could also include II, III, IV, VI, IX or X. Way V (Outsider information) is probably the most time-intensive.

If you can spend quite a lot of time selecting your investments, but then want to spend a limited amount of time supervising your portfolio, the most suitable Ways are III, VI and VII, where, having selected good companies, you can more or less lock them away, with an occasional vault inspection.

5. Range and type of contacts

Some of the Ways (namely I, II, III, IV, VIII, IX and X) can be pursued even if you know nobody in the investment or commercial communities.

The other ways require some personal knowledge of people running businesses, or some detailed familiarity with one industry or type of investment.

6. Financial and quantitative skills

Some investment advisers declare in no uncertain terms that you need to be a financial expert – adept at balance sheets, computers and financial valuation – in order to invest your own money. I do not agree, partly because I have seen many successful investors who would not fulfil these demanding criteria, and partly because it depends on which method you choose to follow.

The following Ways do not require a high level of financial sophistication: I, II, VIII. Additionally, someone who is financially literate but not an accounting expert could practise the following Ways successfully: III, IV, V, VI, IX, X. Only VII really requires a high level of financial sophistication, and my simplified version of this could again be used by someone of intermediate expertise.

But for those of you who are financial whizzes, do not despair. With the sole exception of my Way I, your additional knowledge will prove useful.

7. General personality

This is explored in the next chapter and combined with your type of personal expertise. In some ways your personality should be the most important influence in picking an appropriate investment philosophy. For those who want a taster or a very short summary of the next chapter: if you are a rationalist who weighs things carefully, you really ought to follow one of the more analytical Ways (II, IV, V, VI, VII, IX or X); if you are someone who believes in the primacy of people over calculations, of industrial reality over sentiment, of particular companies over general trends, then your choice should be between III, V, VI, and possibly IX or X; if you are a visionary who likes to take chances with particular choices, the most likely Ways for you are I, II, III, VI, VIII or IX.

➤ Concluding remarks

The folly of trying to fit everyone into a common investment straitjacket should already be apparent. Before moving on to the different investment options, though, let's examine the issue of personality fit more thoroughly.

How to pick your own approach

Practical versus personality considerations

What short of person are you?

Three types of people

Summary of approach suitability

A final word before you read Part Two

PRACTICAL VERSUS PERSONALITY CONSIDERATIONS

You should already have used Chapter 6 to form a shortlist of the possible Ways that are likely to be the best for you, based on practical considerations, like your investment timescale, risk profile, expertise and time available. Chapter 6 also hinted at the question of personality fit, which can be the most important reason for selecting a particular investment approach. This chapter explores the personality fit in much more detail. Quite apart from helping you refine your shortlist, you should gain some insight here into that most elusive and indefinable entity: your character.

> You should gain some insight here into that most elusive and indefinable entity: your character.

WHAT SORT OF PERSON ARE YOU?

The test below should reveal a part of your personality highly relevant to your behaviour as an investor, as well as being of general interest. Harold ('Hal') Leavitt, that great American sage of human behaviour, taught this to me, but no doubt I have perverted his doctrine somewhat, so I apologise to him if this is a garbled version. (The insight, I hasten to add, is his not mine. The specific test below was, however, developed by me without reference to him.)*

---

* For a fuller and more accurate account of Professor Leavitt's views, see his excellent new book, *Corporate Pathfinders*, published by Penguin, London, which I cannot recommend too highly.

THREE TYPES OF PEOPLE

Leavitt categorises leaders into three types. All can be extremely effective (or destructive) but each type leads by quite different means.

Type 1: The visionary

This is perhaps the type of leader most people would expect: bold, charismatic, original, often eccentric, brilliant and uncompromising. Someone who offers a clear break with the present and a dream of what could be in the future. Raiding history's storehouse for examples, Type Ones would include Jesus Christ, Gladstone, Garibaldi, Gandhi, Churchill, Hitler, John F. Kennedy, Martin Luther King, Margaret Thatcher, and the Ayatollah Khomeni. All of these had insights and dreams which were revolutionary; all provided inspiration to their followers; and all were at times extremely impractical and bad at getting things done. After all, what could be less practical than Martin Luther King's tingling declaration, 'I have a dream'?

Type 2: The analyst

This is the leader who is also brilliant, but who deals with numbers and facts rather than dreams and opinions. The analyst is a rationalist who believes that 'if something cannot be reduced to numbers, it is meaningless'. The analyst tends to deal in black and white rather than shades of grey: there is a right answer somewhere, as long as the necessary facts can be collected and analysed. The analyst can use numbers and accounting conventions to control a vast empire in a regular, predictable and understandable way. Business tends to be stocked more with analysts than the corridors of history: examples include two introverts, Clement Atlee and Sir Owen Green, as well as Robert Macnamara, Lord (Arnold) Weinstock, and Harold Geneen. Political parallels would also take in Pitt the Younger, Sir Robert Peel, Harold Wilson, Jimmy Carter and Bill Clinton.

Type 3: The doer

This is the genius of action: the implementer, fixer and successful pragmatist. Generally unencumbered by vision or analysis, the Type Three leader just loves to twist arms, marshall forces, and get things done.

Examples from history include Noah, Attila the Hun, Alexander the Great, Julius Caesar, Louis XIV, Napoleon, Bismarck, Lloyd George, Lenin, Stalin, Eisenhower, James Callaghan, and Lyndon Johnson.

Most people are not 'pure' types, in that they have classic Type 1, 2, or 3 characteristics and none of the others, but all leaders have a dominant streak in one of these three directions that makes them relatively easy to classify. This is also one of those cases where most people are correct in their own self-assessment, so you probably know already to which group you belong. If you are fed up with tests, you may skip the one below as long as you have a firm idea which Type you are and this is supported by asking some friends or colleagues. For the test lover, however, we can make the Type diagnosis below.

THE (1–2–3) TEST

1   *Do you believe in God?*
    (a) Yes (b) No

2   *Do you like saying, 'Bring me Facts, not Opinions'?*
    (a) Yes (b) No

3   *Do you believe there is a right and a wrong answer to most questions?*
    (a) Yes (b) No

4   *Do you prefer thought to action?*
    (a) Yes (b) No

5   *Do you believe in Fate?*
    (a) Yes (b) No

6   *Have you ever been called 'a bull in a china shop' or something similar?*
    (a) Yes (b) No

7   *Do you like using a calculator, and also use one often?*
    (a) Yes (b) No

8   *Do you like poetry?*
    (a) Yes (b) No

9   *Do you like opera?*
    (a) Yes (b) No

10 *Are you more an extrovert than an introvert?*
(a) Yes (b) No

11 *Do you like thinking about philosophy?*
(a) Yes (b) No

12 *Do most people say you are very creative?*
(a) Yes (b) No

13 *Are you PARTICULARLY good at getting things done?*
(a) Yes (b) No

14 *Are you aggressive?*
(a) Yes (b) No

15 *Do you tend to avoid confrontation and argument?*
(a) Yes (b) No

16 *Could you imagine yourself as a politician?*
(a) Sometimes (b) No

17 *Do you prefer dealing with words or numbers?*
(a) Words (b) Numbers

18 *Could you imagine yourself as an accountant?*
(a) Yes (b) No

19 *Do you quite often let your heart rule your head?*
(a) Yes (b) No

20 *Which of the next three characters are you most like (or least unlike)?*
(a) Hitler (b) the Daleks (c) Attila the Hun

Scoring the 1–2–3 test

The way to score the test is unusual. Each question may or may not generate points for you, and there are three different sorts of points which must be scored separately: **Black** points, **Blue** points, and **Red** points. Follow the instructions and tally up each of the points as you go through your answers.

First tally the BLACK points:

Score **10 Black points** for **each** of the following answers: if you answered **(a) to Question 4; (a) to Question 5; (a) to Question 8; (a) to Question 9; (a) to Question 11.**

Score **20 Black points** if you answered **(a) to Question 12.**
Score **30 Black points** if you answered **(a) to Question 20.**
Now add up the total of Black points, which could be between zero (if you did not give these answers to the questions) and 100.

Next, tally the BLUE points:

Score **10 Blue points** for **each** of the following answers: if you answered **(a) to Question 2; (a) to Question 3; (a) to Question 7; (b) to Question 10; (b) to Question 17; (a) to Question 18; and (b) to Question 19.**

Score **30 Blue Points** if you answered **(b) to Question 20.**
Now add up the total number of Blue points, which again will be between zero and 100.

Finally, tally your number of RED points:

Score **10 Red points** for **each** of the following answers: if you said **(b) to Question 1; (a) to Question 6; (a) to Question 14; (b) to Question 15; (a) to Question 16.**
Score **20 Red points** if you answered **(a) to Question 13.**
Score **30 Red points** if you answered **(c) to Question 20.**
Again, add up your total of Red points. This will also be between zero and 100.

Your 1–2–3 profile and what it means

Now, your 1–2–3 profile can be read as follows: the Black points represent your Type 1 score, the Blue points your Type 2 score, and the Red points your Type 3 score. Put them together in this order for your 1–2–3 score.

The highest score represents your dominant trait, and the second highest your secondary trait. For example, a score of 20–60–0 would indicate someone whose main characteristics were Type 2, with a dash of Type 1. Such a person would be very productive in an analytical job which requires a measure of creativity, but which carries no executive responsibilities. A score of 20–10–70 would indicate someone who is a hands-on implementer with common sense and a degree of vision but almost no inclination for theory and numbers. A score of 50–30–0 could belong to someone with a strong sense of vision, and a creative view of how to build for the future, with some analytical inclination, but hopeless at managing people. A score of 90–10–50 would mean someone unusually strong on creative vision, with little interest in analysis, but with quite

> **The test cannot measure one person's actual abilities compared to those of someone else.**

a strong interest in practical implementation. Remember that the absolute scores mean little: it is the relative size of the 1–2–3 quotients that matters. Remember also that we are measuring a person's correlation with a person's relative abilities under the three headings (for the simple reason that it is easier to be good at something you are interested in), but the test cannot measure one person's actual abilities compared to those of someone else. For our purposes, take the highest score only as being relevant, defining your dominant type trait.

Investment implications of your 1–2–3 test score

Table 7.1 gives the best fit of your personality type with the Ways to beat the stock market.

Table 7.1

Way		Type 1	Type 2	Type 3
I	Rainmakers			✔✔
II	Backing winners	✔✔		✔✔
III	Specialisation		✔✔	✔✔
IV	Earnings acceleration		✔✔	✔
V	Outsider information	✔✔	✔✔	
VI	Good business	✔	✔✔	✔
VII	Value investing		✔✔	
VIII	Emerging markets	✔✔	✔	✔
IX	SLITs		✔✔	
X	Warrants	✔✔	✔✔	

SUMMARY OF APPROACH SUITABILITY

We can now summarise the results from Chapter 6 and from the personality test above to check which investment Way is likely to be best for you (see Table 7.2).

The decision tree in Figure 7.1 summarises four of the most important influences affecting your choice of Way, and should lead you to a short list pretty quickly. You might then want to read the indicated chapters first. For those who want an even stronger indication of which Way is suitable,

> You should be pragmatic and only adopt an approach you like, whatever the tests say.

at the cost of grappling with a difficult table, see Table 7.2.

By now you should have been able to 'block in' the approaches which are potentially suitable, perhaps by using a yellow highlighter. You are advised to read these Ways in Part Two before you read the other, diagnostically less suitable Ways.

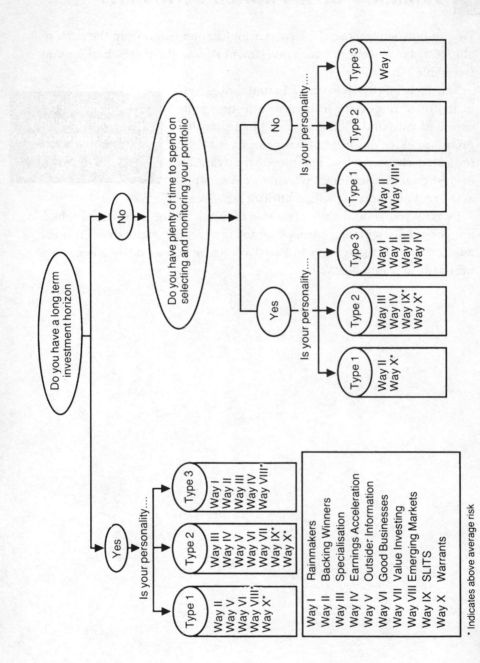

Figure 7.1

Table 7.2

Way	Timescale	Funds	Risk	Time available	Contacts	Quantitative skills	Personality type
I	ANY	ANY	MEDIUM	ANY	ANY	ANY	3
II	ANY	ANY	MEDIUM	MEDIUM	ANY	ANY	1,3
III	MEDIUM OR LONG*	ANY	MEDIUM	MEDIUM OR HIGH	REQUIRED*	MEDIUM OR HIGH	2, 3
IV	MEDIUM OR LONG	ANY	MEDIUM	MEDIUM OR HIGH	ANY	MEDIUM OR HIGH	2,3
V	MEDIUM OR LONG*	ANY	MEDIUM TO HIGH	HIGH	HELPFUL	MEDIUM	1,2
VI	LONG*	ANY	MEDIUM	MEDIUM	HELPFUL	MEDIUM	2,(1,3)
VII	LONG	ANY	MEDIUM	MEDIUM	ANY	HIGH	2
VIII	LONG*	HIGH ONLY*	HIGH*	ANY	ANY	ANY	1,(2,3)
IX	ANY	HIGH ONLY	HIGH*	MEDIUM OR HIGH	ANY	MEDIUM OR HIGH	2
X	ANY	HIGH ONLY	HIGH*	MEDIUM OR HIGH	ANY	MEDIUM OR HIGH	1,2

* indicates particularly suitable in given circumstances

▶ A final word before you read Part Two

The advice and tests above can only be indicative, not conclusive. There is nothing to stop you following any of the Ways in Part Two if you really like it and think it is suited to you, provided you have carefully weighed the words of caution. You should be pragmatic and only adopt an approach you like, whatever the tests say. The one thing you should be very careful about is following one of the higher risk Ways if you have limited resources or a short investment horizon.

Whichever Way you adopt, you should monitor your performance relative to the stock market index closely. This is particularly so if you do choose a Way at variance to those indicated as suitable for your circumstances and personality.

Enough of the trailers! Let's move on to outline our Ten Ways to select shares that perform.

PART TWO

Ten Ways

► that work

> You should select the Way that you like most and which is suited to your personality and skills, and stick consistently to that Way for all your stock market investments.

Introduction

This section introduces you to the Ten Best Ways to investment out-performance with the intention that you should select just **one** approach. All Ten Ways have been selected with the following criteria in mind:

- The Way should have been successfully operated by a number of practitioners with above average results.
- The Way can be described clearly and unambiguously.
- The Way should be a fairly 'pure' approach, that is, not involve a lot of complicated variations or be a blend of more than one investment philosophy.
- The Way should have a clear intellectual foundation, so that it is clear why it can offer superior results.
- The Way should be accessible to individuals without the need for external research or analysis.

There is a remarkable number of possible investment approaches, and in preparing this book I came up with 15 which I considered met the criteria. I then selected the ten which appeared to have the best overall performance on the criteria, taking care to include a variety of Ways so that at least one could be relevant to every private investor, whatever his or her skills, risk profile, time available and personality.

The approaches are listed roughly in ascending order of complexity and expertise required, so that the 'easier' Ways are towards the beginning. What is easy for one person, however, may be difficult for another, so you should pay more attention to whether you could envisage yourself using the approach successfully than to the position in the book. The Ways are **not** listed in any order of overall priority or preference. A brief description of each of the Ways is given in the Foreword (pages ix–xiii) and you may now want to refer to that. The chart below summarises each of the ten Ways according to how simple or complicated it is, and according to the degree of risk. You may use this chart to decide which chapter to read first, or you may want to scan the start of each chapter, which gives a thumbnail sketch of the type of reader most likely to be attracted to the Way.

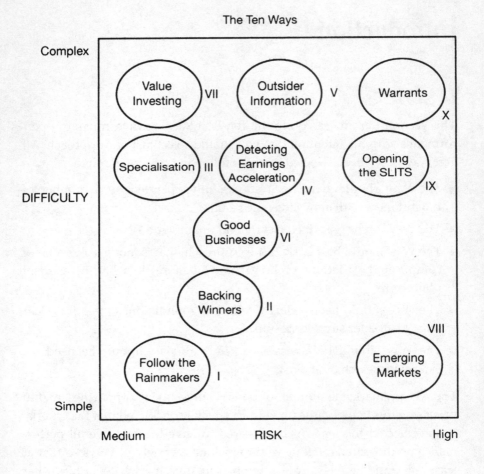

The Ten Ways

Complex

Value Investing — VII

Outsider Information — V

Warrants — X

Specialisation — III

Detecting Earnings Acceleration — IV

Opening the SLITS — IX

DIFFICULTY

Good Businesses — VI

Backing Winners — II

VIII

Follow the Rainmakers — I

Emerging Markets

Simple

Medium   RISK   High

Note that Ways I–VII can be used for the whole of your portfolio, whereas the last three Ways (VIII, IX and X) should only apply to part of your portfolio. Users of any of the last three Ways therefore need to select one of the other Ways to use for the rest of their portfolio, or to 'index track' for the rest of their portfolio instead. Conversely, anyone who selects one of the first seven Ways may also want to devote a small part of their portfolio to one of the last three Ways, to give added spice.

The whole point is that you should select the Way that you like most and which is suited to your personality and skills, and stick consistently to that Way (or two Ways, if including one of Ways VIII, IX or X) for all your stock market investments.

Follow the Rainmakers

This Way can be followed by any investor. It is most suited, though, to Type 3 personalities.

Is investment out-performance a fool's game?

Why the efficient market hypothesis is wrong

Some examples of people who beat the market

How can you benefit?

But is it practical to follow the Rainmakers?

Warning about funds

Beware of new stars

Should you exercise any discretion?

What about following company directors' moves?

Who is this Way best for?

Overall evaluation

IS INVESTMENT OUT-PERFORMANCE A FOOL'S GAME?

You may often hear people say the following:

- 'the stock market is a casino';
- 'it's no use trying to beat the market';
- 'stock market prices are a random walk so it's all a matter of luck';
- 'the market incorporates everything that everyone knows about particular shares and the overall state of industry and the economy, so it is foolish to think that you know better';
- 'the stock market is an efficient market and there are no imperfections to be exploited'.

> The wild swings which are often seen in stock market values are not consistent with a rational examination of fundamental data.

The last two points have even been elaborated into a revered business school academic theory called The Efficient Market Hypothesis, which tends to command sage nods of assent on the business school campus and in the American boardroom. Yet all of these views, whether from the man on the Clapham bus or professors at Chicago or Yale, are absurd and demonstrably untrue.

WHY THE EFFICIENT MARKET HYPOTHESIS IS WRONG

There are two reasons. One is that the wild swings which are often seen in stock market values are not consistent with a rational examination of fundamental data. Crashes like those of 1929, 1974 and October 1987 which wipe 30–70% of value out in a matter of days reflect far more animal spir-

> It is inconvenient for the theory to discover that the impossible actually does happen.

its and the herd mentality than a change in fundamental value. What happened to make shares worth 30% less during the second half of October 1987 compared to the first half? There was a hurricane in the UK, but nothing else had changed: there was no economic crisis, no change in government, and not even the event of the crash itself changed the lives of many people. It must therefore be true that either shares were over-valued before the crash, or under-valued after, or both, rather than being correctly valued both before and after.

People who buy shares when they are 'cheap' – on the basis of Price Earnings or Market-to-Book Ratios – and sell when they are 'dear', consistently make above average returns from their investments. This would not be possible if the market was truly efficient.

The second reason why the Efficient Market Hypothesis is demonstrably wrong is that certain individuals consistently do beat the market. If the whole point of the theory is to persuade people that trying to beat the market is a fool's game, it is inconvenient for the theory to discover that the impossible actually does happen.

The belief that miracles do not happen, because they violate laws of nature, can be undermined if it could be shown that just one person is consistently able to perform miracles. In the case of superior investment performance, it is not just one person, but a whole host of them.

SOME EXAMPLES OF PEOPLE WHO BEAT THE MARKET

They document these things best in America. One particular, small group of investors with a similar philosophy, who were disciples of an investment guru called Benjamin Graham, produced four documented examples of superior returns over many years. These were reported in an amusing article by Warren Buffett in 1985, gleefully proving that miracles could happen. Buffett was one of the four case histories himself, and he has continued to out-perform the market ever since (in 1993, *Forbes* reported that he was the richest person in America, worth £5.5 billion). The evidence was summarised in the following table (Table I.1).

There are a lot of numbers in Table I.1 To put it in perspective, even after the experts running the funds had taken their expenses and profits, $5,000 invested in the average of these four funds would have produced $143,492 in 20 years, whereas the stock market average would have produced only $24,183. The moneymakers, in other words, produced 5.9 times the final return. Buffett himself, as the star performer, would have turned the $5,000 into $357,588 for you – almost 15 times the stock market average final return.

Table I.1   **Four examples of beating the market, 1956–1984**

	1 Fund's annual compound rate of return including dividends	2 Return to investor after management costs	3 S&P 500 annual return	4 Superior achievement (2 minus 3)
Warren Buffett:				
Buffett Partnership Ltd. 1959–1969	29.5%	23.8%	7.4%	16.4%
Thomas Knapp:				
Tweedy, Browne, Inc. 1968 (9 months)– 1983	20.0%	16.0%	7.0%	9.0%
William Ruane:				
Sequoia Fund, Inc. 1970 (from July 15)– 1984 (1st quarter)	18.2%	17.2%	10.0%	7.2%
Walter J. Schloss				
Walter J.Schloss Associates 1956–1984 (1st quarter)	21.3%	16.1%	8.4%	7.7%

Source: Warren Buffett, 'Up the Inefficient Market', *Barron's*, 23 February 1985.

In reality, they beat the market by a greater amount, and creamed a little off for their expenses and profit. Taking Buffett's return on investments before these charges would have turned the $5,000 into a staggering $879,762, or 36 times the market average final position.

Not included here, but cited by Buffett, were other people belonging to the same circle and school of thought – Charles Munger, Rick Guerin and Stan Perlmeter – who also have outstanding long-term records. Not belonging to the Grahamite school, but also consistently successful, have been investors like William O'Neil. More recently, investors of a different stamp, like George Soros, have also built up shorter, but still consistent, records of beating the markets.

In Britain, there are examples of people like James Goldsmith, Christopher Moran, Jacob Rogers, Jim Slater, Sir John Templeton, and Sir John Woolf, as well as unsung heroes, whose long-term records are distinctly superior to the market. This does not mean that they never make mistakes: just that their batting average is high.

HOW CAN YOU BENEFIT?

The principle is obvious. If certain individuals or their funds consistently beat the market, get on their coat-tails. If you can find out what they are buying and selling, do likewise. Particularly if you lack time or expertise yourself, this is a very simple investment philosophy to adopt: Follow the Rainmakers.

BUT IS IT PRACTICAL TO FOLLOW THE RAINMAKERS?

If it was totally easy and straightforward, perhaps more people would adopt this approach, and market imperfections might become somewhat smoothed, to the astute investor's disadvantage. But it is not as difficult as you might think to follow the Rainmakers. Some rules and procedures which help include the following.

1. First, choose your Rainmaker. You could adopt any of the names mentioned here, or any other individual you come across (it could even be

a friend or acquaintance) who has a distinguished record. But first of all, ensure that you have documentary proof of the superior performance from a reputable source or from first-hand inspection of the records. It is a good idea to choose a Rainmaker (like Buffett and his friends) who has a long-term investment philosophy and does not 'churn' investments frequently, as this will both keep expenses down and make your job of tracking the investments easier.

> ..... Choose a Rainmaker who has a long-term investment philosophy and does not 'churn' investments frequently. ....

Newsletters are sometimes a good source of Rainmakers. Newsletters vary enormously in quality but, perhaps surprisingly, some are very good. The two that I like best in the UK are *The IRS Report* (where I have been a contributor) and *The Investors Stockmarket Weekly*.

2. Once you have chosen your Rainmaker, stick with him or her. Do not exercise discretion or change horses in mid-stream.

3. Find out if the Rainmaker operates a fund. If so, the easiest (although not necessarily the most profitable) thing to do is to join the fund. Check the record of the fund again first, however, and make sure that the fund is not committed to keep most of its investments in any particular sector (see the 'Warning about funds' below).

4. If the Rainmaker does not operate a fund, or if you don't want to pay the fund's charges, establish where and how you can find out about purchases and sales. Jim Slater, one of the Rainmakers, writes a regular column in *The Independent*, so is easy to follow. Another Rainmaker who is easy and worthwhile to follow is Kevin Goldstein-Jackson, who writes an amusing 'Diary of a Private Investor' every weekend in the *Financial Times*. If there is a fund, it will publish an annual report with its largest holdings listed, but that may be out of date. The best source is stock exchange announcements about significant holdings, or financial newspaper reports of these or of purchases and sales of stock. These reports will probably be a few days old, and you may have to pay slightly more than the price paid by your Rainmaker, but if the holdings are kept over a fairly long period this will not matter too much. Alternatively, you could have a rule that you will not pay more than, say, 3% or 5% above the Rainmaker's entry price, so that you either wait for the price to settle back to this level or, if this never happens, you pass on that particular investment. Be sure to monitor sales as closely as you monitor purchases. It is probably not wise to wait to

sell after the Rainmaker has exited the stock, even if you have to take a lower price.

WARNING ABOUT FUNDS

The comments above about consistent track records refer mainly to individuals, and relatively small or entrepreneurial funds associated with individuals, rather than to the biggest British or American investment institutions. In the absence of other data, choosing a fund based on its historical track record is not a bad idea, but big funds which have done particularly well often have a nasty habit of reversing this out-performance at some point. This is partly because they are wedded to a particular sectoral weighting, and inevitably sectors have their ups and downs, if only because of the fashion element in general stock market valuations. The other main reason for lack of sustained out-performance by funds is that they tend to invest in a large number of shares at any one time, which makes serious and prolonged out-performance less likely.

BEWARE OF NEW STARS

Do not select as your Rainmaker someone who has come to prominence recently and whose track record has not been (or cannot be) checked further back. You should avoid anyone who has a short-term record or whose gains are associated with just one type of investment (like gold, or recovery stocks) which have benefited from a cyclical revaluation. This type of Rainmaker, however spectacularly successful in the recent past, may be heading for a very dry spell.

SHOULD YOU EXERCISE ANY DISCRETION?

What happens if your chosen Rainmaker takes a position in a company which you believe has poor prospects? Should you pass on that investment, or continue to follow the Rainmaker despite your personal doubts? Or, what if the Rainmaker sells shares which in your opinion still have a lot of mileage in them?

You should have no hesitation in buying and selling the same shares as your expert. In fact, if you are liable to have doubts or want to second-guess the Rainmaker, you have probably chosen the wrong Way to beat the market! If you exercise discretion you have undermined the whole basis of this particular Way: you would be mixing two different approaches and would have no rational

> .... **If you are liable to have doubts or want to second-guess the Rainmaker, you have probably chosen the wrong Way to beat the market!** ....

basis for deciding when to back your own judgment and when to follow the expert. Exercising even the tiniest bit of discretion is the thin end of the wedge. No, you must follow the Rainmaker religiously, until and unless you decide that the approach is not working and decide to abandon it.

WHAT ABOUT FOLLOWING COMPANY DIRECTORS' MOVES?

One intriguing variant of the 'Rainmaker' approach is to follow company directors when they buy or sell shares in their own companies. Instead of following one individual Rainmaker, you would be following the judgment of insiders in a number of businesses.

Information on directors' sales and purchases is reported to the stock exchange and published by the exchange at once. A useful summary – although a week out of date – is published in the second section of the *Financial Times* each weekend. A specialist service can provide this information rather more rapidly.

The theoretical attraction of following directors – who should know what is happening in the company – is obvious. Despite this, the evaluation of this method by objective academics, both in the UK and the US, shows very mixed results, depending on the time period and exact methodology taken. If any general lesson is to be drawn from the research, it is that directors are on average good at deciding when to sell, but not convincingly above average in their purchase decisions. Certainly the evidence of directors' wisdom is less convincing than one would expect.

We can only speculate on why directors do not make stunningly good buy decisions. To some extent their view of the firm may be too insular, not taking sufficient account of competition or overall factors like the economy as a whole, and tending to believe the firm's propaganda too much. The average performance is also weighed down by particular examples where a few directors of companies in trouble, like Maxwell Communications or Polly Peck, publicly bought their shares in a futile attempt to shore up confidence and the share price ahead of a collapse.

It is also difficult to discriminate between cases where the directors are buying or selling shares for personal reasons – such as to increase their degree of personal control, or to meet a tax bill – and those cases where they really do know something material about the company's prospects. The information published will tell you the amount of money involved, but not the net worth of the director concerned (and therefore not how important this transaction is to the individual).

Information on directors' trading is always interesting. It is possible that a selective approach to directors' transactions would provide a good way to beat the market. Unfortunately I have not yet been able to isolate such an approach.

Advantages... *of following the Rainmakers*

This approach has much to commend it:

1. Certain individuals who are long-term investors do consistently beat the market. Getting on to their coat-tails is a sensible objective.
2. Once you have found your Rainmaker, and identified how to shadow his or her transactions, this is a relatively easy Way to follow. It requires no special contacts or analytical skill, only discipline in following the Rainmaker's investments.
3. After the initial identification period, this Way also requires relatively little time.

Disadvantages... *of following the Rainmakers*

There are two major problems with this approach:

1. You need to identify your individual to follow. This is easier to do with confidence in respect of US investors, where the track record is easier to document. But to follow US investors properly, you need to follow their investments in the US, which you may not want to do, and which

in any case adds to the cost and difficulty involved. There are some suitable UK investors but you will need to check their records carefully.

2. You will need care and skill in identifying how exactly to track your individual's trading. You will need to be diligent in following the moves quickly and accurately.

WHO IS THIS WAY BEST FOR?

This approach does not require any special skills or contacts; it is not particularly time intensive; it does not need a high-risk profile; and it is suitable for any size of investor. Like all the Ways, it is better to have a long time horizon, but shorter-term investors are not debarred from this Way.

In personality terms, this is not really suitable for most Type 1 or Type 2 people (see pages 69–77 above). If you are a Type 1, you will probably want to make your own decisions or at least exercise discretion on which investments to follow, so you

> This Way may be an exception, in offering high returns for relatively modest effort.

will not find the automatic nature of this Way attractive. If you are a Type 2, you will want to do your own analysis and this method gives no scope for this. If you are a Type 3, the no nonsense, practical nature of this method will probably appeal.

Although this is in many ways an 'easy' method (after the 'set up' period), I am convinced that it is a very attractive one. It should therefore not necessarily be eschewed by the sophisticated investor, who could choose to execute one of the more difficult Ways. A Type 3 sophisticated investor might like this approach and actually find it more profitable than some of the more difficult Ways which follow. Generally, efforts and reward are closely matched; this Way may be an exception, in offering high returns for relatively modest effort.

▶ Overall evaluation

The tremendous returns which could have been had over at least three decades by following an investor like Warren Buffett speak for themselves. If you have the skill and patience to identify your individual (or are happy to follow Buffett's primarily US investments) and the ability to find a simple way of tracking the investments, this is a very attractive method.

The difficulty is in the practical mechanism to do this. In the UK it is not at all easy to find individuals with proven records or to get timely information on their moves. In some respects, this Way may be slightly ahead of its time. But as disclosure requirements become more stringent and information is provided more quickly and cheaply, as will undoubtedly happen in the future, this Way will become easier and more reliable to follow. (For any entrepreneurs reading this who are also well versed in City ways, this may be a good service to consider supplying.) In any case you may know an individual who does have a good track record and would let you know his or her moves, or be happy to make largely US investments. But, if you cannot see how to make this Way work, or if it is too passive a method for you, fear not: there are nine other good Ways to beat the market coming up.

WAY 11

Backing winners

This Way is relatively simple, although it does require daily share price monitoring. It is best suited to Types 1 or 3 personalities.

GOOD AND BAD INVESTMENTS

If you chose a portfolio of shares at random, locked them away, went abroad and came back 30 years later, you would certainly find some things to surprise you. Let us imagine the grand day, say on your 70th birthday (you can adjust for your real age now) when you open the safe, identify the shares and their cost, and, perhaps with a slight tremor, hold the latest *Financial Times* in your hand. One other thing you do before opening the *FT* is to calculate the real cost adjusted for 30 years' inflation of the investments, so that you could fairly compare the cost to the prices in this future edition of the paper. Before you finally open the paper and learn the fate of your investments, you write down your expectation of how they have done. What would you guess?

Most people would expect something like the following:

- a bunch of investments, perhaps the majority, have done slightly better than inflation;
- one or two real winners which have done exceptionally well;
- one or two real losers that have lost most of their value.

Yet, this would probably be wrong. Based on past simulations, the most likely outcome would be rather different:

- a large minority (say 35–45%) of the investments would have done very well, and beaten inflation by a very large margin (a guess for illustrative purposes might be an average of 10% per annum better than inflation, which would compound to give terrific performance);
- a similar large minority of shares would have done rather poorly, perhaps only keeping up with inflation or even falling a bit behind;
- there would be a few real star performers with brilliant performance;
- one or two of the shares would be nearly or totally worthless.

WHAT'S THE DIFFERENCE?

Most people would expect a central bunch of shares with broadly similar performance. Analysis suggests a much more biblical picture: that of the sheep and the goats. And the interesting thing is that this tends to happen over a long time period. Somehow, shares seem to divide into those that do well and those that do less well over the long term.

> Once a company is good or bad it is likely to remain so.

You can probably corroborate this to some extent from your own experience. If you follow the record-keeping procedure recommended in Chapter 5, and rank your investments by monthly, quarterly or annual relative performance, you are likely to find many of the same names keep cropping up at the top and bottom of your list.

There is evidence to suggest that this happens particularly *within* a given industrial sector (like pharmaceuticals or stores). Of course, there will be cyclical swings in the fortunes of any given sector. But there will be some companies who do better than their competitors and out-perform their sectoral index, and they are more likely to be the same companies over long periods of time.

THE LAW OF GOOD AND BAD BUSINESSES

This states that there are good and bad companies, and therefore good and bad shares, and that once a company is good or bad it is likely to remain so. Of course, there are exceptions. Some bad companies become good, and some good companies become bad. Yet these are surprisingly rare.

This is all against our natural instincts of fair play, supporting the underdog and a place in the sun for everyone. It is unegalitarian. But it does seem to happen.

WHY DO GOOD BUSINESSES STAY GOOD, AND BAD BUSINESSES, BAD?

I am speculating, but I think I know why. The truth, I believe, is that it is very difficult to change the direction and fortunes of large companies. I have studied attempts to 'transform' large British and American companies from 1970 to 1992, that is to cause a step function change in the way that they do business and their level of financial returns. The interesting result is that about three-quarters of all such attempts to redirect companies ended in failure.

I conjecture that there are two basic reasons why it is difficult to change companies. One is that they are often locked into a competitive structure which it is difficult to change. Often a competitor has a real edge in terms of market share and size, brand, technology, service levels or some other structural advantage that it is expensive, difficult and possibly even futile to fight against. The British motor-cycle industry disappeared against assault from Japanese companies like Honda and Yamaha, and once these companies had reached a certain size they could simply make better and cheaper machines so that there was almost no financially viable strategy for the losing British companies. Similarly, American Motors and Chrysler suffered a scale disadvantage when compared to Ford or General Motors, and were therefore doomed to inferior returns in the mass market.

Companies are difficult to turn around, except in extreme crisis, because they tend to have cultures and ways of doing business that are very difficult to change.

You can probably think of many other examples from your own experience, where whatever a company does, or whatever whizzkid it appoints, it is structurally at a disadvantage and likely to remain so. Michael Edwardes had a high reputation when he was appointed boss of Chloride, but it was a 'bad company' and resisted all Edwardes' skills aimed at reviving it. Similarly, even the great troubleshooter himself, Sir John Harvey-Jones, could not arrest the decline of the Burns-Anderson Group when he was appointed its deputy chairman. Warren Buffett himself hit the nail on the head. 'When a company with a reputation for incompetence,' he declared, 'meets a new management with a reputation for competence, it is the reputation of the company that is likely to remain intact.'

The second reason for the persistence of 'good' and 'bad' companies relates to their insides, not to their competitors. Companies are difficult to turn around, except in extreme crisis, because they tend to have cultures and ways of doing business that are very difficult to change. Think of all the effort that has gone into improving British Rail, and how disappointing the results are. Under-performing companies tend to have undistinguished staff, low relative efficiency, little sense of direction, poor morale, and relatively low staff commitment to the firm or its customers. Such companies find it difficult to attract the best recruits available to their industry, or to learn better ways of doing business as fast as others.

The result is that 'good' companies with strong competitive positions and cultures, like Marks & Spencer, will probably always be good long-term investments, whereas companies with a poor record of earnings growth and share performance are more likely than not to continue down a disappointing track. There is undoubtedly a Darwinian element to the stock market: survival of the fittest is the most likely outcome.

TWO WAYS TO EXPLOIT GOOD BUSINESSES

By now you are probably tired of this lecture on good and bad businesses. What on earth, you may be muttering, does this have to do with beating the stock market? My answer: a great deal. In fact, there are two different ways of beating the stock market which can follow from the Law of Good and Bad Businesses:

1. Identify a few good businesses, and invest in them for the long term.
2. Follow a System which, over time, limits the downside from mistaken investments and maximises the return from good investments.

This chapter deals with the second way – the System – while Way VI explores how to find good businesses, not just by looking at historical performance, but by capitalising on your own knowledge, experience and skills.

BASIC PRINCIPLES OF THE SYSTEM

These are very simple:

- Select initial investments with a history of good long-term performance.
- You will still make mistakes in selecting your investments.
- The easiest and best indicator of such mistakes is a price decline.
- Sell your worst shares early and with limited losses.

- Hang on to your best performing shares.

The philosophy behind the System is one of profound respect for the stock market and what it is telling you. Good shares will go up and bad shares will go down. If the market is sending a share down, it is probably bad and has further to fall.

The System holds that this is true both in the long term and the short term. Shares start to fall because the most alert or well-informed investors start to sell. As others catch up with the information, the shares will fall further. The fact of an incipient fall should therefore be given prompt attention. Similarly, but in reverse, a share that starts to rise often does so because the most astute investors realise it is undervalued, so the signal given by the rise should be given due weight.

The System I have devised to reflect these principles can be followed precisely and mechanically by anyone who is reasonably disciplined and can read the *Financial Times* each morning. I will explain what to do, and give more detail on the underlying philosophy, as we go through each of the propositions listed above.

SELECT INITIAL INVESTMENTS WITH A GOOD TRACK RECORD

Your objective should be to pick ten shares with a good historical track record. For example, Table II.1 shows the ten best-performing shares from the FT 30 index, over the period from 1982 to 1992.

Table II.1

Company	Share price (pence) Jan 1982	Jan 1992	Value of £100 invested	Annual rate of return %
1 Glaxo	27	853	£3,868	44.1
2 Guinness	32	508	£2,244	36.5
3 Tate & Lyle	48	401	£1,263	28.9
4 Hanson	24	200	£1,173	27.9
5 Courtaulds	60	505	£1,166	27.8
6 Reuters*	196	1527	£872	24.2
7 Grand Metropolitan	68	441	£858	24.0
8 BTR	44	237	£742	22.2
9 Cadbury Schweppes	85	425	£710	21.6
10 ICI	144	595	£652	20.6

* June 84–September 93

The best six performers' share prices over this period are shown in Figures II.1–II.6.

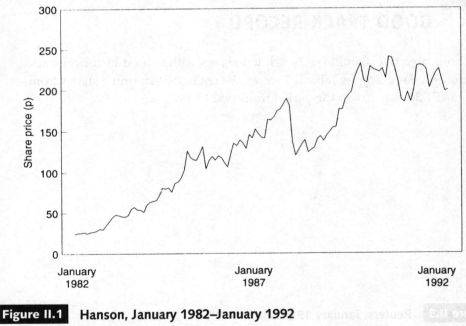

Figure II.1   **Hanson, January 1982–January 1992**
   Source: Datastream

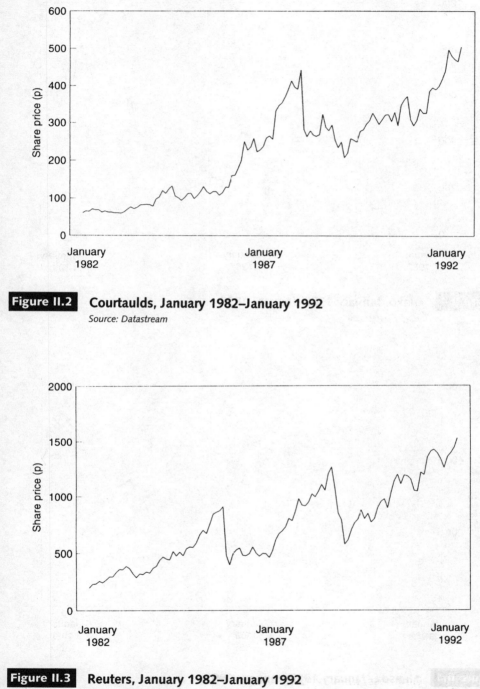

Figure II.2 **Courtaulds, January 1982–January 1992**
Source: Datastream

Figure II.3 **Reuters, January 1982–January 1992**
Source: Datastream

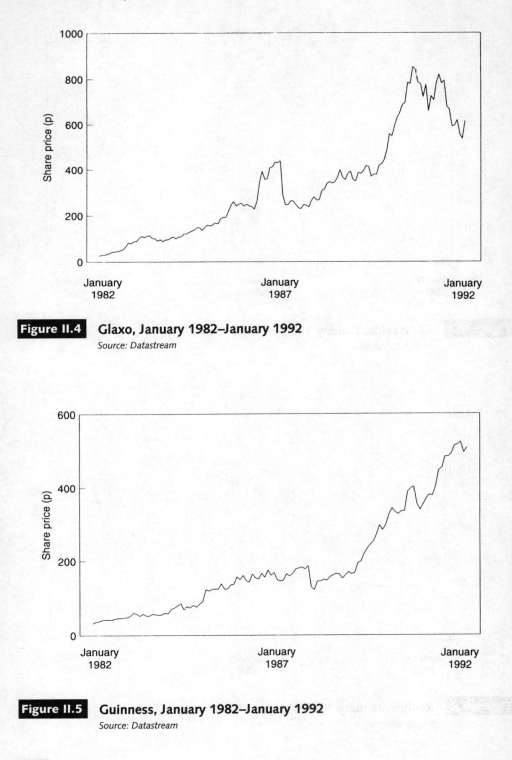

Figure II.4 **Glaxo, January 1982–January 1992**
Source: Datastream

Figure II.5 **Guinness, January 1982–January 1992**
Source: Datastream

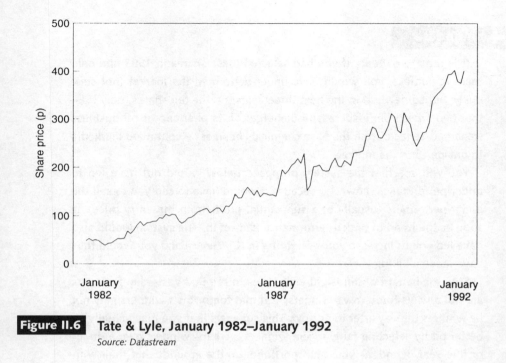

Figure II.6 Tate & Lyle, January 1982–January 1992
Source: Datastream

Ideally, in selecting your shares, you should get an up-to-date table of the best performers from the FT 30 index or the FT-SE 100 index over the past five or ten years. Your stockbroker should be able to provide this, or you may see something similar in a newspaper or financial magazine. Note, though, that the list must be up to date, and if it is even a few months out of date it is not good enough: if a share has under-performed badly in the past few months, this may be an indication of a longer-term decline.

➜ an update

It is time to own up. If you had selected these shares in 1993 and held them regardless, you would have under-performed the market (not seriously, but somewhat) in the next three years. Of the ten shares, only ICI – that benefited from a successful demerger of its pharmaceutical business (renamed Zeneca) from the base chemicals business – continued markedly to out-perform the market.

You will see that the system proposed below would not have led to under-performance, however, because it would have forced you to sell the under-performers (usually at a substantial profit from the entry price) as soon as the trend of under-performance had set in. The system would also have led you to increase your weighting in ICI/Zeneca and you would thus have made a killing.

Still, the benefit of hindsight enables us to see that yesterday's winners are not always tomorrow's winners, and that tomorrow's winners may not be winners the day after tomorrow. This suggests that you may actually be better off by selecting fairly recent winners, perhaps winners over a three- or five-year period, as your start portfolio, on the grounds that their winning run probably has longer to go.

There is another fascinating suggestion: that the starting portfolio does not much matter. The system may well work well on a purely random selection of shares.

A DIGRESSION: THE O'HIGGINS RULE

At the risk of complicating things a little, let me introduce you to an alternative way of selecting your starting shares which can be undertaken at the start of any calendar year. This method was pioneered in the US by Michael O'Higgins where it has achieved above average performance over the past ten years; a simulated exercise using the FT-SE 100 index has recently indicated that it would have also out-performed the market.

The O'Higgins Rule is three-fold:

- select the ten highest yielding shares in the index
- then pick the five with the lowest share price

• repeat the exercise every year

I find the empirical evidence of out-performance quite persuasive, but I do not believe in magic rules, and am not convinced that there are adequate reasons explaining why the O'Higgins Rule should work. I respect the results to date, but am not wholly convinced that the Rule will work in the future.

➜ an update

I was right. The Rule performed badly in 1994 and 1995. For late 1996, as I write, it is still unclear. Perhaps 1997 and 1998 will prove better for the Rule.

If you like the Rule, however, and prefer this as a method of selecting your starting shares, it can be slotted into the overall System explained here quite neatly. I will refer to the alternative procedure for followers of the O'Higgins Rule as we progress. You should bear in mind, however, that if you follow the Rule you will only have five shares in your portfolio, which will increase the risk a little.

CORRECTING YOUR MISTAKES AND LIMITING THE DOWNSIDE

The System relies upon active trading of your shares, and in particular the elimination of under-performing shares. The rule is to sell your worst shares first. This is the opposite of the commonly practised, but generally pernicious, practice of 'averaging down', which we deplored earlier (pages 40–42).

The System is simple. If your shares start going down, this may be the start of a big decline, and may indicate that the company is going to experience long-term difficulties. This may, of course, not be the case: the market may be reacting to insignificant short-term news, or a large seller may have temporarily upset the market, or there may be a thousand and one innocent explanations. Nevertheless, the System says: you cannot afford to take the risk. There are many examples where shares, including those that have performed healthily in the past, start to fall, and where those who ignored the market's hint suffered heavy losses.

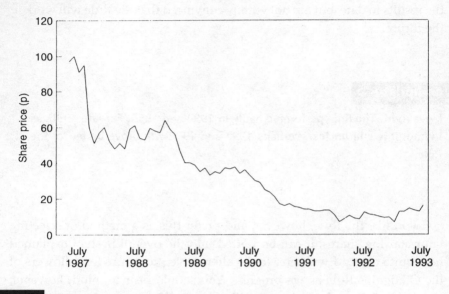

Figure II.7 Chloride, July 1987–September 1993
Source: Datastream

The case of Chloride (see Figure II.7) marks a classic pattern. As the graph of its share price from 1987 to 1993 shows, the generally downward trend here would have been ignored at the investor's peril, despite the frequent recommendations of share tipsters who claimed repeatedly that the corner had been turned.

The System therefore dictates that *you should sell any share on which you have already sustained a loss of 8%* (ignoring stockbrokers' commission). If you buy at 100p and the price falls to 92p (a fall of 8%) you should automatically sell. In order to be sure of doing this, you should keep a close eye on any share which is showing a loss. Even if the market itself is declining, you should stick to this policy (the market itself may fall further, too).

The logic behind the System is simple too. Only a few investments will prove to be really big winners … but if you stick with them, you will make excellent returns from them. The investments which could potentially cancel out these stars are losses on the big losers, of which there will be a few ... unless *all* losers are nipped in the bud, before they can cause real damage. A successful American investor, Bernard Baruch, put it this way: 'If a speculator is correct half of the time, he is hitting a good average. Even being right three or four times out of ten should

> .... **If you start to show small losses, cut them at once before they have the opportunity to turn into big losses.** ....

yield a person a fortune if he has the sense to cut his losses quickly on the ventures where he has to be wrong.' Therefore, if you start to show small losses, cut them at once before they have the opportunity to turn into big losses. You may be wrong about some of these, but your mistakes will never cost you large sums or depress your overall performance average too badly.

You may feel reluctant to take losses on some shares. The shares you started with will have an excellent history. You may feel strongly that the market has got it wrong, and that the underlying quality of the firm will shine through in the share price sooner or later. To tell the truth, you may feel emotionally committed to the buy decision you made. You may hate to realise a loss and pay all those transaction costs, *but accept no excuses, and make no exceptions*. A loss is a loss, and must be cut when using this Way. If you think you may find this difficult to do, don't try to follow this System. If you ever break any of the System's rules, you are on your own again. The System can only work like a computer or a Vulcan, without emotion or discretion.

HOLD YOUR BEST-PERFORMING SHARES

The System would not work unless you do show some substantial gains from the 'good' part of your portfolio. In order to allow these gains to materialise, you have to be patient. The theory enunciated above would seem to suggest that for the really good companies, you should be prepared to hold the shares almost for ever. You should be just as slow to take your profits as you are quick to limit your losses.

SUPERSTARS AND MINI-STARS

If you start with ten shares and play the System for ten years, it is likely that you will only end up with one, or at the most, two of your original selections at the end. Yet the chances are that you will make up to half or even more of your total profit out of your one or two shares representing only 10% or 20% of your starting capital. It is also likely that the bulk of the rest of the gains will come from a number of 'mini-stars' held for average periods of say 2–3 years, and showing an average return of 25% per annum over that period.

Let me illustrate this with some notional numbers which again illustrate the power of compounding (Table II.2)

Table II.2

Year	Mistakes £	Mini-stars £	Superstars £	Total £	Increase %
Start	50	40	10	100	
End 1	46	50	14	110	10.0
End 2	42	62	20	124	12.7
End 3	39	78	28	145	16.9
End 4	36	98	39	173	19.3
End 5	33	122	55	210	21.4
End 6	30	153	77	260	23.8
End 7	28	191	108	327	25.8
End 8	26	238	151	415	26.9
End 9	24	298	211	533	28.4
End 10	22	373	295	690	29.5

✳ **EXAMPLE** Assume that you have just one share that compounds in value over ten years at 40% per annum (some examples of such performance are given below). Assume also that just 40% of the portfolio on average has been invested in the 'mini-stars'. Finally, assume that *all of the remaining portfolio, that is, half of it, has been invested in mistakes, which get sold each year at an 8% loss.* You might guess that having half of the portfolio in mistakes would sink its performance. But the numerical example below shows that this would not be the case. Let us assume we start with £100 capital.

These calculations do illustrate certain key points:

1. The superstar ends up increasing in value from £10 to £295 and at the end comprises almost 43% of the total value. If the superstar had been sold during the first five years, the overall portfolio performance would not have been good. If there had been two such superstars, they would have ended up dominating the portfolio, and it would not have mattered hugely what happened to the rest.
2. If at the end of year 1 a brave decision had been made to 'average up' the superstar position, and invest a further £14 at that stage (another 12.7% of the portfolio, so that just over a quarter was invested in the superstar), the total return would have been hugely better.
3. The mini-stars are vital to the overall performance of the portfolio. A proven mini-star should therefore not be sold, because it can be difficult to generate replacements. On the other hand, if the performance of any mini-star starts to deteriorate, it is necessary to sell it in order to hold up overall performance.

We should not, perhaps, make too much of an illustrative set of numbers. In practice it would not work out like this, for two reasons. First, it is highly unlikely that half the original portfolio would turn out to be absolute losers: year on year losses have been very unusual, and are almost inconceivable over ten years for a sample from the FT 30 index or the FT-SE 100 index. Much more likely there would be a tail of mediocre performers. Secondly, it would be difficult to reinvest all the mini-star money, when some mini-stars eventually had to be sold, in another set of mini-stars, rather than a random selection of good and bad performers. It is much more likely that the whole process would be repeated year by year, whereby we hit upon one superstar, a few ministars, and the rest under-performers or losers. These two differences of reality from the simple model above might or might not cancel each other out, so Table II.2 can hardly be regarded as realistic, even though it should have focused your mind on the importance of fully backing the winners.

FULL SYSTEM RULES

The full proposed System rules are:

1. If any share has shown a gain of 40% or more during its first year in the portfolio, buy an equal value to its current value, provided that this

does not take the total weighting of one share in the portfolio over 25%. Sell other shares to finance this transaction, starting with the worst performers (in percentage terms) and carrying on until you have the necessary funds. If the weighting subsequently goes above 25% because of appreciation, do not worry, but do not buy any more. *Those investors who are particularly risk averse should NOT follow this 'averaging up' rule, which increases the degree of risk.*

2. Monitor your superstars (i.e. any share showing an annualised return of at least 30%) carefully, and sell half of the total of any superstar that has declined 15% in value from its peak value. If it then declines another 15% (from the level when you sold the first tranche) sell the remainder.

3. Hold your mini-stars (i.e. any share that shows an annualised return of at least 20%) as long as they keep rising. If any mini-star shows a decline of 7% from its peak value, sell half. Sell the other half if there is a further fall of 7%.

4. Sell all of any other share that declines by 8% from its purchase price, or by 10% from its peak value, whichever happens first.

5. At the end of each year, sell any share that has not realised a gain at least equal to the average of the FT 30 or FT-SE 100 (depending on which index you used in starting the portfolio).

6. If you have new funds to invest (net of any reinvestment in the superstars), aim to 'top up' the portfolio so that there are ten shares in it at any one time (do not worry if there are periods when there are only between five and nine shares in the portfolio, but try to get back to ten when this can easily be done). In choosing new shares, you should apply the same criteria as when you started, but using updated data.

7. Finally, note that the rules above are not designed to deal with 'meltdown' conditions of a stock market crash or a prolonged and severe bear market. Since this is a mechanical System, there must be a rule for dealing with such conditions. The rule is: if the stock market index you used to help select your starting investments declines by 10% or more from its level when you started, or by 15% from its previous peak, *sell everything*. Put the money in an instant access high interest account (currently in Britain the best rates for these are with certain building societies: choose one of the larger ones that does offer a rate near to or above the bank base rate). Then wait until the index has gone up by 10% from its recent low, and buy the same number of shares in all your previous portfolio companies, regardless of whether this level is high-

er or lower than that at which you sold (it should normally be lower, but do not fret or hesitate if it is not: just buy).

A DIGRESSION ON 'NEW HIGHS AND LOWS'

This is not strictly related to the System, but one of the most interesting parts of the financial press is the column of 'new highs and lows' reached in the year by individual shares (for example, this occurs on the back page of the markets section of the *Financial Times*). The interesting thing is that if you read the whole column or just one industrial sector of the column for several days running, you often find the same company names recurring. In other words, a share making a new high often then makes another, and another, while a share making a new low often achieves that dubious distinction several times too.

A share making a new high often then makes another, and another, while a share making a new low often achieves that dubious distinction several times too.

What is particularly interesting is to look at the column of New Highs on a day when the stock market generally has done poorly. This is often a pointer to further progress on the way (and the reverse is often true for shares hitting new lows on days when the market has done well). Whereas it is usually a bad move to buy when the market as a whole is hitting new highs, it is usually a good move to buy when an individual stock is hitting a new high in a weak market. As so often in life, what looks expensive may prove to be cheap, and what looks cheap may prove to be over-valued.

✔ Advantages... *of the System for backing winners*

The System has four clear advantages:

1. The initial selection of stocks that have performed well over long periods is a sound basis for selection of a portfolio.
2. The System is biased towards 'listening to the market', which is generally a more reliable and less risky approach than approaches based on the opposite philosophy.

3. The System recognises that mistakes are inevitable – even the most experienced and successful professional investors make lots of mistakes – and limits the loss from any mistakes.

4. The System is simple to operate and does not require any special expertise or contacts.

✗ Disadvantages... *of the System for backing winners*

There are also four drawbacks which should be pointed out:

1. Although the System is based on some very sound principles that have been around for a long time and been followed by successful investors, the System itself is a new distillation of rules invented by the author, and has not been tested and validated in its current form.

2. Any automatic System cannot operate inexorably and successfully for ever. The stock market is not susceptible to magic systems, and the proposed System may or may not produce above average results. Do not be deceived by the apparent precision of the rules and the confidence that this may induce. The System is only a mechanical interpretation of certain investing principles.

3. Any System should be followed mechanistically without discretion. Particularly for sophisticated investors, the System may constrain skills you have learnt and the temptation to deviate from the rules may at times be overpowering. If you are a sophisticated investor and you do deviate, make sure you do so in the form of new rules that you write down (and please let me know about them, if they prove in practice to be an improvement!).

4. Whereas this System may generate above average returns, it is intrinsically unlikely to generate huge returns, unless you are lucky enough to pick a few exceptionally good superstars. This is because the risk aversion rules and the 'listening to the market' will tend to put you off one of the best ways of making a killing, which is to invest **against** the consensus of the stock market in a company that you know is undervalued. I believe it is quite possible that the System may produce long-term returns of 5% or so above the market average (which when compounded for a while will make a very significant difference), but it is unlikely to generate returns of say 20–30% above the market average each year, which some of the riskier methods discussed later have the potential to do.

WHO IS THIS WAY BEST FOR?

This approach is perhaps best for the interested and keen novice, rather than a very experienced investor, someone who is an expert in a relevant area, or anyone who has limited time to monitor their investments. The Way does not require special skills, but it does take time to monitor percentage changes in the performance of shares, so anyone who cannot read the financial press daily should not pick this Way.

In personality terms, there are two groups for whom this Way is probably **not** suitable:

> The Way is therefore a good introduction to the stock market for those who are interested but inexperienced.

- Those of an analytical cast of mind may like the precision of the Way, but are likely to want to reach their own view of the merits of shares based on fundamental analysis, rather than relying on any system. On the whole, therefore, this Way is not recommended for 'Type 2' readers (see pages 69–77).

- People who are basically rebels and non-conformists will probably not like the way in which the System is skewed towards the market trend. They may feel that the System kow-tows too much to the short-term conventional wisdom of the stock market. So if you are the sort of person who goes racing and backs outsiders rather than favourites, this Way is probably not for you.

➤ Overall evaluation

The rules do embody a lot of shrewd market wisdom (gathered, I hasten to add, from others who have spent their lives trading). The Way is therefore a good introduction to the stock market for those who are interested but inexperienced. It is particularly useful in warning against errors that most newcomers make, like averaging down and trying to fly in the face of a strong market flood (Canute is the patron saint of inexperienced and unfortunate investors).

The System requires you to spend some time monitoring the market and your investments, but is straightforward and does not require expertise. It is unproven in its current form but not particularly risky. At the very least, it provides a good starting philosophy for the new private investor.

WAY III

Specialisation

This Way requires time and some special skills. It is suited to personality Types 2 and 3.

Know few things well

Successful investors specialise

Where are you an expert?

Assessing your true expertise

Overall evaluation

KNOW FEW THINGS WELL

One of the great, universal laws of life is specialisation.

This is how life itself evolved, with each species seeking new ecological niches and developing unique characteristics. This is how guerilla warriors like the Viet Cong defeated the might of America, or the Afghans drove the Red Army out. This is how business opportunities arise, where instead of tackling a competitor head on in his 'power alley', clever newcomers go round the edges, finding new segments and attacking laterally on a narrow front. This is how Apple outwitted IBM, by focusing on personal computers; how IKEA broke into the furniture market, by specialising in high design but self-assembly furniture; how Marks & Spencer broke into food retailing, by concentrating on a small range of high-quality convenience foods; and how countless small businesses take on much larger and better resourced ones. A small business that does not specialise will die. One that does specialise may grow rapidly and earn better returns than a broader-based established concern.

It is the same with investment. It is better to know a few things well, or one thing very well, than it is to know everything superficially. This is where many investors, both individuals and fund managers, go wrong. They think it useful to read the financial press from cover to cover, to keep abreast of trends in the economy, in technology and in management. They believe in having a broad spread of investments in different industries, locations, and types of company. But they must be information processing geniuses or extraordinarily insightful to keep up with all this data **and** know more that matters than the specialist. The plodder who knows one area backwards will nearly always out-perform the brilliant generalist.

SUCCESSFUL INVESTORS SPECIALISE

Examine almost any successful investor, and you will find that he or she tends to specialise in one way or another: in bonds rather than equities, in

> **Defining your strongest suit or best future area of investment focus may take some reflection.**

precious metals, in exotic countries, in particular industries, in developing companies, in currencies, or in particular instruments such as convertibles, options or warrants.

Warren Buffett, for example, has made most of his money out of industries he knows intimately, especially media and financial services. Sir James Goldsmith would like to have done the same, but knows most about the food industry and has made the most impressive returns there. Lord Hanson is very clear about his area of focus: basic businesses, with relatively stable technology, where one person can take responsibility for success or failure. His acquisitions follow a consistent pattern over several decades of targeting under-managed, under-performing businesses of this type, stripping away the fat and unnecessary assets, and imposing personal accountability and financial discipline on them.

WHERE ARE YOU AN EXPERT?

Most people shy away from the tag, 'expert'. But if you were not an expert in something, it is unlikely that you would have generated surplus funds for investment or be reading this book! And even if you believe you are not yet an expert in a particular investment area, you could set yourself the task of becoming one.

Defining your strongest suit or best future area of investment focus may take some reflection. Areas that you consider as possibilities include the following:

1. Your industry (in which you work).
2. Other industries.
3. Your professional or functional skill.
4. Your region.
5. Your hobby.
6. Retailers.
7. New issues.
8. Developing quoted companies.
9. Recovery stocks.
10. Acquisitives.

Let's now consider which of these specialisations is best for you.

1. Your industry

If you work in a specialised industry, like insurance, banking, aerospace, automotive, retailing, wholesaling, cosmetics, mining, oil, or many, many others, this may be a good basis for your invest- ment specialisation. The first requirement, how- ever, is that there be a number of relatively 'pure', quoted companies operating in your industry. It's not much use if you're an expert in the pet food industry, for example, because the largest compa-

> Investing in your own business should ... be approached with care

ny (Pedigree Petfoods) is a private, unquoted concern, and the others are part of larger quoted companies where the pet food side is not dominant. In insurance, on the other hand, nearly all the large companies are quot- ed 'pure plays' (although one of them, Eagle Star, is just part of BAT Industries).

If you work in an industry with a number of quoted 'pure' plays, this is good news. Now ask yourself the following questions:

- Is it likely that I will come across news relevant to the industry's future prospects, or realise the significance of such news, ahead of the brokers who specialise in following the industry?

- Similarly, will I become aware of 'leading indicators' of one particular firm's impending success before others do? Such leading indicators include: market share gains, breakthroughs in technology, attracting above average recruits, and so on. These indicators are 'leading' because they do not instantly translate into improved earnings, but are likely to over the medium and long terms.

- Will I be able to objectively and accurately assess the quality of management, and particularly new top management, before it is apparent to the world at large?

- Will I be able to use any such useful information legitimately, without being in any danger of 'insider trading' or breach of my fiduciary responsibilities to my employer?

The last consideration is, or course, crucial. It may be advisable to eschew investment in your own business, or at least to apply to yourself the same stringent rules that directors of the company have to follow (if in doubt ask your compliance officer, company secretary, or finance director). Investing in your own business should also be approached with care for two other reasons: the danger of putting too many eggs (your money and

> The only word
> of caution is that you
> should not invest too
> heavily before
> you really are
> an expert!

your job) in the same basket; and because you may not be objective about your company and may put a blind eye to its vulnerabilities.

Even if it is not your own company, you may be in possession of inside information, as a function of your job. Again, if in any doubt, seek formal advice from your firm. In general, you should not use information about specific events which are likely to, or may, affect the share price in the short term. This is, in any case, a precarious basis for an investment. Much more valuable is insight into longer-term trends which could change the pecking order or profitability in the industry. Such insight is unlikely to constitute insider information as legally defined, but (if you are right) will certainly have a major impact on future valuations.

2. Other industries

There is no necessary reason to confine your industry specialisation to the area where you work, provided you start out with a reasonable knowledge base in the other industry. For instance, your father may have been a printer and you may have always been interested in the printing and publishing industries, even though you work as a doctor. Or you may harbour an ambition to retire and run a hotel or a leisure park, and be slowly building up relevant expertise. Perhaps you know a number of people in the media, and decide to specialise in evaluating the ITV franchise companies.

Whichever industry you select, you must start with a deep interest in it and some base of knowledge or contacts. You can gradually build up more detailed knowledge of the industry and the quoted companies in it. The only word of caution is that you should not invest too heavily before you really are an expert!

3. Your profession or functional skill

Your vocational skill may cut across several industries, yet still be relevant for investment purposes. Say that you are an expert in materials technology, or in marketing, or in executive search (headhunting). You must then consider how your expertise might help you select individual companies for investment purposes. The materials technologist may gain an insight into a new component that will dramatically lower the cost base of certain manufacturers. The marketing expert will be able to evaluate the prospects for certain brands, or see where a new product could revolutionise the prospects for a small company. The headhunter may know that there is a cultural revolution afoot in Timbuctoo Airways that will transform its prospects.

To some extent such insights occur by luck. But do not overlook the extent to which your expertise can be deliberately harnessed and channelled to gain insight into particular companies.

A good exercise here is to force yourself to write down a list of the 10 or 15 quoted companies where it is more likely that your functional expertise could yield such insights. Then think about how you can improve your understanding of what is going on in each of these companies and its competitors. You may be surprised at the potential for insight into their prospects. Like anything else where you wish to build up expertise, however, it takes application and effort. Decide where to make this commitment, keeping it focused wherever possibly in narrow limits. Deep expertise in relation to a few companies is much better than less deep knowledge regarding many companies.

> Deep expertise in relation to a few companies is much better than less deep knowledge regarding many companies.

4. Your region

Geography is a much overlooked basis of expertise. You have a particular advantage if you live outside the M25 area, or the Home Counties generally. It is remarkable how far City opinion and share prices are influenced by perceptions formed in London and the South East, which may be quite atypical of the country as a whole. For example, City analysts have recently concluded that the opportunities for further expansion by the big supermarkets like Sainsbury and Tesco are few and far between. Consequently, the rating of these companies have been high. The perception of market saturation in food retailing is true in the South East, but not in the country as a whole: yet Home Counties provincialism rules the roost.

You can turn this 'M25 Myopia' to your advantage. If you live in the West Country, you might choose to specialise in, say, a dozen of the quoted companies based in your area, particularly those which do a large part of their business in the area. The same applies if you are based in Wales, the Thames Valley, East Anglia, industrial Lancashire, in the North West,

North East, or Scotland. You may be part of or have access to the top industrialists or commercial people in your region. Even if you are not, you should be able to use contacts or some rationale to build such a network.

As before, your aim should not be to make a fast buck by accessing short-term, price-sensitive information. Instead, you should spot certain trends and leading indicators before the impact they will have is factored into share prices in the right measure. Be on the look out for the rapidly expanding small local firm which has discovered some neglected niche or a superior way of doing business. Work out whether its formula could be 'rolled out' on a national basis. Make a shortlist of the companies where local knowledge is likely to be crucial to medium- and long-term share valuation, and then cultivate knowledge about them. Work at building your expertise. If you are a long way from London, and work diligently in your chosen field, you may reach a level of insight which it would be difficult or impossible for City analysts to match.

> Spot certain trends and leading indicators before the impact they will have is factored into share prices in the right measure.

5. Your hobby

One of the most pleasurable forms of investment specialisations is in an area which is already known to you because it is your hobby. True, few investors are so lucky, but it is worth considering whether you could be one of the few.

For people living in Britain, one of the most obvious areas is that of the regional brewers like Boddington, Fuller, Greene King, Morland or Young. Including the cider companies, there are, in fact, 16 such regional companies listed daily in the *FT* (and a number of others that aren't), most of whom are only in two businesses: brewing and owning/running pubs. If you are an analyst who is not averse to real ale or visiting the pub, becoming an expert on regional brewers may not be the most arduous of tasks.

In similar vein, the restaurant industry also offers some potential. Fast-expanding chains like PizzaExpress, Pelican (that runs the Cafe Rouge chain) and Harry Ramsden's (fish and chip restaurants) offer the ability to conduct market research in (for some) conducive surroundings.

The leisure sector also offers a large number of football clubs (though it is only the large ones like Manchester United, Millwall and Tottenham Hotspur that are quoted daily in the *FT*) and racecourses (none quoted daily, I very much regret), as well as a number of other peculiarities.

The media sector also offers some interesting stocks, including local radio (Capital, Southern Radio and others), many TV stations, and a host of newspaper companies.

The 'Miscellaneous' section in the *FT* includes a number of curiosities, including toy manufacturers (Bluebird and Hornby), games manufacturers (JW Spear), and household names in their sector like Christies and Sothebys, Colefax and Fowler, British Bloodstock, Photo-Me, and many others. If your hobby is shopping, the stores sector offers specialists like Body Shop, Liberty, MFI, Reject Shop, Tie Rack, and the World of Leather, as well as the big chains. Finally, there are companies like Filofax, Regina, and Boosey & Hawkes that will be familiar to people with certain lifestyles and hobbies.

> ...... **The correct way to view a hobby is as a jumping-off point for serious study of a company.** ......

It should be pointed out that there are three potential drawbacks to a focus on 'hobby' investments. One is that if this is your only area of investment, you will be unduly exposed to sector risks, and you really should therefore limit any leisure investments to a maximum of 25% of your total portfolio. You will therefore need another basis of specialisation as well.

The second drawback is that many of these shares are in companies with low total value, which can make them difficult and expensive to trade in, as well as volatile when there is a burst of buying or selling. This does not matter so much if you are a long-term investor, or if you are really confident that you have identified value not recognised by the market. The third drawback, however, relates specifically to this point as well. Beware lest your enthusiasm for Fuller's ales, for example, blinds you to any business vulnerabilities that may exist, or stops you selling when your analysis says you should.

The correct way to view a hobby is as a jumping-off point for serious study of a company, with incidental benefits in terms of your starting knowledge and fun, rather than as an extension of the hobby itself.

6. Retailers

This is worth mentioning as a separate category even if you don't like shopping. One of the great advantages of retailers is that they are transparent to the private investor. If you invest in British Aerospace, for example, you will find it difficult to arrange a visit to their defence establishments so that you can check out what is happening – but anyone can walk into Asda, Marks & Spencer or Moss Bros and check how busy they are, whether the staff are motivated, and what new products they are selling. Not surprisingly, one of the keys to success in retailing is buying and merchandising, and you can form a first-hand assessment of relative performance here by visiting several competing retailers and see who has the better value, design or appeal to particular customer groups.

7. New issues

A different type of specialisation is to focus on particular types of shares or stages of their existence. New issues – that is, buying shares the first time they are offered to the public – is an interesting specialisation, and can be a very profitable one. In contrast to the advice almost everywhere else in this book, this method is suitable for investors with a very short time horizon, although it can be interesting for someone with a long horizon also. Table III.1 list the new issues from June 1993 to May 1987.

New issues fall into two broad categories: those issues by the government in privatisations and similar flotations; and those where private companies are coming to the market for the first time. They have somewhat different characteristics. Not to put too fine a point on it, the government-sponsored issues tend to be underpriced, and often come with incentives for the private investor, and positively discriminate in your favour and against the investment institutions in terms of allocation of shares and sometimes even price. Whether you view this as a commitment to popular capitalism or a vote-grubbing exercise does not matter.

> .... **The greatest annualised returns on investment generally go to those who sell shortly after the new issue.** ....

The greatest annualised returns on investment (although not the absolute amount of profit) generally go to those who sell shortly after the new issue. If there are a lot of a new issues pending, profits can then be rolled over into the next privatisation. Alternatively, they can be held for a longer time, until or beyond the availability of the incentives.

There may not be many new privatisations or further new issues in existing privatised companies (like BT) coming up in the near future, although Rail and Coal are clearly pending. On the other hand, for investors willing to take an international perspective, there are many foreign privatisations (many in 'stable' countries like France) which are likely to show the same concern to give private investors and good deal, and it may be possible even for foreigners to invest in some of these. One possible strategy is to buy such shares in the open market shortly after they have been floated, when the excess of small shareholders cashing in their profits may lead to the shares still selling below their true value.

The second category of new issues is where growing companies float for the first time. It takes a bit of practice and work to ensure that you are aware of all such flotations (publications like the *Investors Chronicle* are very useful here), but all you will need is a good stockbroker who is on the ball and can obtain stock for you (some flotations are 'private placements' which are not advertised to the public at large). To my knowl-

> **Always read the prospectus carefully and form your own judgment.**

edge no definite research has been published on the relative profitability of new issues versus contemporaneous investment in the stock market as a whole, but it is clear that many new issues are somewhat underpriced, and you can always pick and choose between available new issues.

Underpricing in the non-government new issues can occur for several reasons. Except in rampant bull markets, the sellers of the business will be willing to take a little less than it would normally be worth just to get their hands on a quote and/or large amounts of cash. The stockbrokers and bankers responsible for the flotation will want to give themselves an easy job in getting the shares underwritten and sold. Both groups (advisers and owners) will want to ensure a 'healthy after-market', that is, that the shares are seen to perform well in the period following flotation, and the best way to do this is to underprice in the first place.

If you are following new issues carefully, you should be able to weigh the respective merits of a number of issues coming to the market at the same time or shortly after one another. Always read the prospectus carefully and form your own judgment. If at all feasible, do this before you read the opinions given in the financial press and by stockbrokers, although you should recognise that the latter often become self-fulfilling in the short term. Unless you are a short-term 'stag', however, only invest in new issues which you personally think are good value for the medium and long term. Before long you will begin to get feedback on your decisions.

Table III.1

Company	Launch date	Issue price (pence)	Price at 29/10/93	Annualised growth rate %
Northern Ireland Electricity	18/06/93	220	324	189.3
National Express	09/12/92	165	257	64.7
Powergen	11/03/91	175	462	44.5
South Wales Electricity	10/12/90	240	671	42.8
Seeboard	10/12/90	240	669	42.6
Manweb	10/12/90	240	667	42.5
Norweb	10/12/90	240	655	41.6
Northern Electricity	10/12/90	240	651	41.3
Yorkshire Electricity	10/12/90	240	640	40.4
Midlands Electricity	10/12/90	240	630	39.7
Southern Electricty	10/12/90	240	624	39.2
Southwestern Electricity	10/12/90	240	621	39.0
National Power	11/03/91	175	417	39.0
Eastern Electricity	10/12/90	240	613	38.4
London Electricity	10/12/90	240	608	37.9
East Midland Electricity	10/12/90	240	588	36.4
Northumbrian Water Group	12/12/89	240	673	30.4
Welsh Water	12/12/89	240	658	29.7
Wessex Water	12/12/89	240	637	28.6
Scottish Power	17/06/91	240	416	26.1
South West Water	12/12/89	240	580	25.5
Scottish Hydro-electric	17/06/91	240	411	25.5
Southern Water	12/12/89	240	574	25.2
Yorkshire Water	12/12/89	240	553	24.0
Thames Water	12/12/89	240	544	23.5
Severn Trent	12/12/89	240	542	23.3
North West Water	23/12/89	240	530	22.6
Anglian Water	12/12/89	240	521	22.1
British Airways	10/02/87	125	378	17.9
British Telecom	30/11/84	130	462	15.3
British Gas	05/12/86	135	345.5	14.6
National Freight Consortium	03/02/89	263	417	10.2
British Petroleum	30/10/87	330	349.5	1.0
British Steel	28/11/88	125	129.5	0.7
Rolls-Royce	19/05/87	170	153	−1.6
Average annualised share price growth				33.8%
Median annualised share price growth				30.4%

One major reason for specialising in new issues and one of your major tasks will be to develop good intelligence on the new issues coming up and find ways of getting yourself the shares you want. As mentioned above, in many cases this can only be done through the sponsoring stockbroker, so you will need to develop relationships with several stockbrokers. This is easier, relative to your resources, if you concentrate all or most of your available funds on new issues.

8. Developing quoted companies

As with countries, 'developing' often means small and under-resourced. I use the term here, however, in its literal sense, to mean companies that although small are growing rapidly. (I do not include here big companies that are growing rapidly – a rare but possible event.)

There are four reasons for taking an interest in small but fast-developing companies. One is that small companies are definitely different from the larger companies, not just (to adapt F. Scott Fitzgerald's comment that the rich are different because 'they have more money') because they are smaller, but in their ways of working and their managerial requirements for development. The second reason is that it is much easier for small companies to grow fast over several years than it is for large companies, so the potential for capital gain for the long-term investor is often much greater than with small companies (the potential for sustaining a total loss is also much greater). The third reason is that it is often possible to spot accelerating earnings before the implications of this have been factored into the share price, and this is easier to do with small companies. The fourth and related reason is that small companies are often much more accessible to the interested and empathetic private shareholder than their larger counterparts.

The problem for the entrepreneur arises when the business gets too big or complex to be managed inspirationally.

Let's examine these reasons and their implications a little more. Nearly all companies start because someone has a bright idea and goes into business to realise it. This person, the entrepreneur, combines three roles: the inventor/enthusiast/inspirer; the owner; and the manager. Such a person is not, generally, a professional manager who has worked in conventional management roles – that is one reason why he or she still has the imagination to think of a totally new approach. The problem for the entrepreneur arises when the business gets too big or complex to be managed

inspirationally: when it requires professional discipline, people management, and all those difficult and boring things that experienced managers
do. This happens at a turning point in the company's history which can be
defined objectively, and often recognised more easily from outside the
venture than from inside. It happens when **either** the headcount goes over
100 **or** the turnover goes above £20m. At this stage the company, whether
it knows it or not, faces a choice. The entrepreneur can either step aside
(becoming life president or non-executive chairman, taking charge of new
product development, or simply go sailing round the world) and bring in
good professional management with a flair for smaller businesses, or the
entrepreneur can just carry on as before, heedless of any change in the
firm's character.

I can hear some readers muttering that this excursion into the theory of
small firms is all very well, but what does it have to do with making
money on the stock market? The answer very often is: everything.
Because it frequently determines whether the company continues to grow
(indeed, often takes off on an even faster growth curve), or whether it
starts to run into major problems. *And the interesting thing is that you can
spot this before the stock market value implications are built into the share price.
Let's take an example.*

✳ EXAMPLE An entrepreneur has the idea of providing exceptionally fresh and
high-quality sandwiches and salads in a much more attractive,
light, Continental-style setting than the neighbourhood sandwich shop. She
opens her first outlet and it catches on. Soon large queues are beginning to
form, starting at 11.45am. She takes over the next door premises and eliminates
the queues, but ends up with a very profitable business. She then opens another outlet, which also prospers, and before long has a chain of ten, each generating about £1m per year turnover and £250,000 pre-tax profit.

She then floats the company, Sexy Sandwiches, on the stock market. She
opens another ten outlets which perform up to scratch. In its first full year after
flotation Sexy Sandwiches makes another £2.3m pre-tax profit, and has earnings after tax of £1.5m. The company is valued at £15m, and is therefore on a
price earnings multiple of 10 times historic profits. This is below the market average of 15 times earnings, because the market has doubts about the company,
given its short track record and single product focus.

You model the performance of the company, do some site inspections which
convince you that the new outlets are slightly bigger than the old ones, but at

least as full of customers, and work out that in the coming year Sexy Sandwiches might make £4.5m pre-tax (£2.9m after tax), based on having 20 outlets each contributing £250,000, less £500,000 for central costs. This would put the company on a very low prospective price earnings ratio of 5 times earnings (the market value of £15m divided by the earnings of £2.9m), and could thus represent very good value.

Before making your investment, however, you wisely talk to two experts in the industry, both of whom claim that the company is running into management and logistical problems. According to your contacts, the entrepreneur could cope with buying for a small number of outlets, but simply cannot supervise a larger number of suppliers and the higher volume of raw materials needed. Apparently there have been instances of running out of some items and, even more seriously, quality problems with a few salads.

You decide to investigate more carefully, and manage to talk to some of the middle level and junior people at the head office. Some of them are indiscreet, and you get a picture of total disorganisation, disarray and bickering. You begin to wonder about your financial calculations, which were very 'top down' and assumed you could simply extrapolate profits from the earlier experience on a per outlet basis. Perhaps the low stock market value is correct after all!

So far you have put a lot of work in, and made no investment. You might, therefore, conclude that you have been wasting your time. This would be a wrong conclusion. You have saved yourself from making a potentially disastrous investment, and there is no better use of time!

You move on to other things, and while you are reading the *FT* you notice a very small item in the appointments column saying that the founder of Sexy Sandwiches has retired and that a new chief executive, with a very successful track record of running a chain of fast food restaurants, has been appointed. You revisit the head office, find things humming and everyone running around with a sense of quiet purpose. You check with your industry experts who say they believe the new chief executive is on top of the previous difficulties. You decide to make a significant investment in the shares.

When the next annual results are announced, Sexy Sandwiches has after-tax earnings of £2.4m, and margins are significantly higher in the second half than the first, and back up to the margin level of the previous year. Since the firm is still opening a number of new outlets, and your research continues to show no problems, you decide to hang on, even though the historic PE ratio has now risen to the market average of 15 and the total value of the company has increased from £15m to £36m, so that your shares have more than doubled.

In the next year the company had an average of 30 outlets open throughout the year and made £250,000 from each outlet, less central costs of £650,000, for a profit of £6.85m before tax and £4.45m after tax. Seeing that it is a growth stock, the market decides at long last to award an above average multiple of 20 times earnings, for a total market value of £89m. At this stage your investment has appreciated 494% in just over two years.

This example is hypothetical but there are plenty of real-life cases. The next chapter is devoted to a much more detailed examination of how to identify fast-developing companies. Real-life examples are given where earnings acceleration *preceded* rapid share price appreciation. These examples include Pelican (a company with some similarities to the mythical Sexy Sandwiches), Micro Focus, Kwik Save and Filofax (see pages 147–149).

> If you are one of life's optimists you should skip . . . any investment in recovery stocks.

Tracking down companies can be very lucrative, provided you watch carefully for the key management transitions and do your homework carefully. Note, however, that these are big 'ifs', and require an active, investigatory approach as well as careful analysis, before you make your investments.

9. Recovery stocks

Specialisation in 'recovery stocks' is another possibility, but only for the analytically astute and professionally sceptical. If you are one of life's optimists you should skip both this section and any investment in recovery stocks. The sad fact is that many of them never recover.

A recovery stock is one that used to be successful but has fallen on hard times, so that the share price is now a fraction of its highest level, and which someone claims is about to recover. Do not be attracted to recovery stocks because the price has come down and you hope could go back up to the former level: the price has fallen for real reasons and the previous high is now totally irrelevant. Also remember that however low a share is, it can halve in price again, and again, and again …

You may have gathered that, in general, I am not a great fan of recovery stocks. But they are a legitimate specialisation for the sophisticated investor, because they do have certain common elements that repay study. The key thing to realise is that most recovery stocks are still in a downward momentum, or at best 'bumping along on the bottom'. The companies involved have generally suffered a traumatic shock in the form of a market collapse, attack from better competitors, internal feuds or some other disaster. They are likely, therefore, to have a poor reputation with customers, demoralised staff, and weak finances. For these companies to recover requires a major reversal in momentum based on a radical change in real-world conditions. Such favourable discontinuities for troubled companies are fairly rare.

The rule I have adopted (through, it has to be admitted, sometimes painful experience) is: **never buy shares in a 'recovery' company until it is clear that it has begun to recover.** This does not mean that the shares have to have started to creep upwards again, or that this is necessarily an indicator of real recovery in the firm itself. What it does mean is that you have to have firm evidence, based on first-hand investigation, that the company really has begun to put its troubles behind it.

There are, of course, examples of recovery stocks that have recovered and made money for the brave investors who realise a recovery is underfoot. Two recent British examples are Hillsdown Holdings and British Aerospace. As indicated above (pages 31–32), both of these were solid companies where the stock market over-reacted to unexpected bad news following rights issues. In the case of Hillsdown, the shares were punished severely despite the company being profitable and paying a high dividend – for a while the dividend yield was higher than the Price Earnings ratio! On any objective criteria the shares were very good value at anything under 140p, yet they crashed to below 80p in July 1992. Once they started to recover, however, they rapidly surged back towards the 140p level (see Figure III.1). British Aerospace is a good example of a very large company whose valuation reached 'disaster scenario' levels when there was very little chance of the company going bust. From a low of around £1 in mid 1992 the shares quadrupled in four months, reaching a much more realistic valuation (see Figure III.2).

Before you invest in purported recovery stocks, you must have satisfactory answers to the following questions:

- What real event has started the recovery and how has it been able to reverse the downward momentum?
- Do customers share the view that the company has reformed itself and is now a good supplier?
- Is there appropriate new management, including a new chairman or chief executive (there are very few examples of real recoveries without

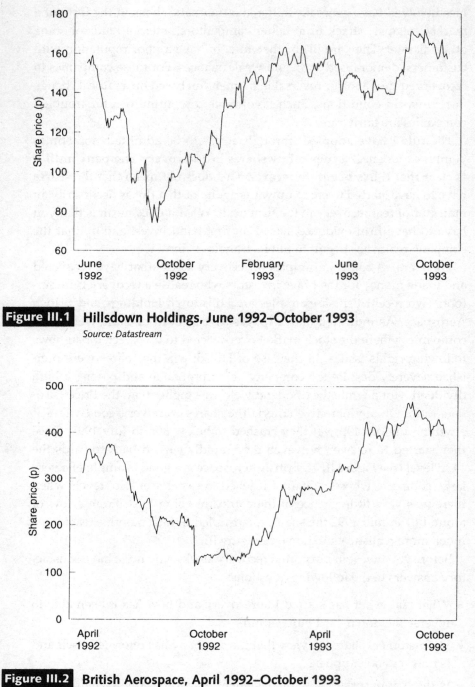

Figure III.1 **Hillsdown Holdings, June 1992–October 1993**
Source: Datastream

Figure III.2 **British Aerospace, April 1992–October 1993**
Source: Datastream

such a new ingredient, although a new boss is not a sufficient condition at all for recovery)?

Making a speciality out of recovery stocks is a difficult and dangerous way to invest, though it can be rewarding for those who are willing and able to undertake primary investigation.

10. Acquisitives

There is a special class of companies which grow mainly by making acquisitions, and add value by spotting good ones, and changing the performance of the acquired companies by various means. Such companies are a legitimate specialisation, but again only for advanced investors.

A recent study by OC&C Strategy Consultants showed that in the UK market between 1984 and 1992 the following large companies were the most acquisitive: AAH, Amstrad, APV, Argyll Group, BBA Group, BET, BTR, Cookson Group, Costain Group, Fisons, FKI, GE, Guinness, Hanson, Hillsdown, Ladbroke, Lasmo, Mowlem, Pearson, P&O, Rank, Ratners, Siebe, Smiths Industry, Smith & Nephew, Tate & Lyle, TI Group, T&N, United Newspapers, and Wolseley. The same study showed that the 'Acquisitives' grew sales, profits, and earnings per share faster than a comparable group of 'organic' (i.e. less acquisitive) companies between 1984 and 1992 and had higher average return on equity (21% versus 15% for the 'Organics'). However, despite performing better, the Acquisitives had a lower stock market rating (in terms of price earnings ratios and premium of market-to-book value for any given level of return on equity) since 1990. Interestingly, this was a reversal of market sentiment between 1985 and 1990, when the Acquisitives, deservedly, were at a rating premium to the Organics.

The market's conventional wisdom has moved against the Acquisitives, despite their superior performance, for a number of reasons, including adverse publicity surrounding the difficulty in making acquisitions, a few spectacular failures of acquisitive companies (such as Polly Peck), concern about accounting conventions that favoured acquirors but are now being tightened, and concern about the predominance of some high-profile chiefs. OC&C Strategy Consultants concluded, however, that in the next few years the Acquisitives were likely to return to favour.

If OC&C is right, this creates a favourable backcloth for a study of Acquisitive companies. One possibility here is to focus on a narrower

> If you are not really an expert in your chosen area, you are likely to under-perform rather than out-perform the stock market.

group of 'Super-Acquisitive' companies within the Acquisitive group, comprising the following: BTR, Hanson and Tomkins (not in the OC&C study). All of these companies add value by the way they pick new takeovers and by the cost-cutting and other controls they install once the acquisitions have been made. A careful study of these companies, comparing and contrasting the value they add and their stock market ratings, could potentially highlight investment opportunities.

ASSESSING YOUR TRUE EXPERTISE

The ten specialisations discussed above, or any others you can think of (and there are many others, including technology shares, 'green' shares, and so forth), all require real expertise. In contrast to the three Ways discussed earlier, they do not lean at all heavily on ready-made solutions or algorithms derived from market experience. Put bluntly, if you are not really an expert in your chosen area, you are likely to under-perform rather than out-perform the stock market. Arrogance could severely damage your wealth. So, if you are thinking of following one of these specialisations, you are strongly recommended to apply four tests:

1. Ask yourself how far you really are an expert, and how your experience and skills are likely to compare with the opposition, that is, fund managers and analysts who may also be specialists.
2. Repeat the exercise, but ask the opinion of some honest friends, so you have some objectivity.
3. Conduct a trial period, preferably without actually making the investments, but noting what you would have done had it not been a trial, to make sure that it works, and that you are beating the stock market index.
4. Continue to monitor your performance each quarter against the market index, and stop if you turn in two consecutive quarters of below average performance.

▶ Overall evaluation

Specialisation is an invaluable concept, and in one sense it applies to all of the Ten Ways in this book. The particular types of specialisation discussed above may or may not appeal to you. None of them are at all easy to execute well, but if you are appropriately confident and competent, any of them can lead to sustained and increasing out-performance.

WAY IV

Detecting earnings acceleration

This Way requires some basic knowledge of accounting and some quantitative skills, as well as time to apply them. You must also be willing to accept some risks. It is most appropriate for Type 2 and 3 personalities.

How the stock market values a company

How do companies attract a high price earnings ratio?

Market values, shares and earnings per share

So what?

Does re-valuation of a share happen overnight?

How to back the horse after the winning post

Why do PER changes lag earnings rises?

What sort of earnings growth are we looking for?

Identifying prima facie 'accelerators'

Verifying the history

Assessing future profit trends

The investment decision checklist

Multiplying your money

Predicting profit growth before it materialises

Who is this Way best for?

Overall evaluation

HOW THE STOCK MARKET VALUES A COMPANY

What is a company worth? If you were sitting on a desert island thinking it through from first principles, you might invent 1,001 ways to value a company, and you might have a hard time deciding which way was best. You might or might not include the one way that most analysts, stockbrokers and investors use as the single most important measure of a company's value: multiplication of a company's profits after tax ('earnings') by an 'appropriate' price earnings multiple.

It is fascinating to see the complexity of all companies in all industries operating in any country around globe and quoted on any stock market reduced to this single measure of performance. Once you understand this measure, you can use it to target where there might be returns well above the market average.

Very simply, the stock market takes the earnings of a company and then multiplies them by a number called the 'price earnings ratio' (abbreviated here to PER, though it is often simply called the PE) to arrive at the value of the company.

Consolidated Gasworks (CG plc) has reported profits after tax ('earnings') for the year to 31 December 1993 of £80m. What is the total value of the company?

EXAMPLE ✳

Value of CG plc   = Earnings *times* PER
                  = £80m x ?

The magic ingredient for valuation is the price earnings ratio. What should this be? It is usually a number between 5 and 25, but the astute mathematician will quickly spot that this could place a value on CG plc of between £400m and £2bn, which is quite a wide range. If you were a shareholder in CG plc, you would want to know where in the range it came!

This is where valuation leaves science well behind and becomes a black art. Analysts never appear in doubt as to what PER is appropriate. But the way they judge it is to compare with other similar companies or with the stock market as a whole, and then look at the relative prospects for growth in the earnings, which is a sensible method but rather circular. The circularity in the argument and potential volatility in the PER both offer huge profit potential for the astute investor. But we are in danger of getting ahead of ourselves. It is important first of all that you understand how analysts judge the PER and the intuitive logic behind this method of valuation.

> The idea of valuing a company by taking a multiple of its earnings makes intuitive sense.

HOW DO COMPANIES ATTRACT A HIGH PRICE EARNINGS RATIO?

The idea of valuing a company by taking a multiple of its earnings makes intuitive sense. If you assume that earnings translate into cash (which is broadly correct), you could imagine someone being willing to pay several times the earnings now in a lump sum payment to buy a company, in order to enjoy the cash from the earnings each year. If our mythical investor was willing to pay ten years' worth of today's earnings now in order to enjoy the earnings (whatever they are) of the company for ever, then the company would be valued at ten times earnings.

The investor would not do this if he or she believed that the earnings would not last long or would decline from today's level – it would be foolish to value a company making hula hoops at ten times earnings if the earnings were in a boom period when there was a fad for hula hoops, but were expected to last at most for a year or two. A hula hoop company might deserve a PER of only 1 or 2 (times earnings) on this basis.

But what if the investor expected the earnings to go up? What if the company made a product where the demand was expanding rapidly, like semiconductor chips in the 1960s and 1970s or Filofaxes in the 1980s, and the company had a history of increasing earnings? In these circumstances it would be logical for someone to pay a higher PER to buy the company, perhaps 20 times earnings. If Accelerated Earnings plc is making £1m a year in earnings, but you know that it will be £3m in a couple of years' time, a 30 times PER (that is, valuing the company at 30 times this year's earnings or £30m) will translate to a 10 times PER in two years' time (£30m divided by £3m), which might then seem a very modest valuation if the earnings are still rising at all.

Analysts sometimes talk about the 'prospective' PER, that is, the price earnings ratio next year or the year after, assuming certain projected earnings for that year. In the case of Accelerated Earnings plc, the prospective PER in two years' time would be 10, which would mean that paying a PER of 30 now would not look so frighteningly expensive.

THREE EXAMPLES: PER VALUATIONS

EXAMPLE ✳

To complete this prologue, imagine three companies: Slow Lane Industries plc which has completely flat earnings (the same every year); Modest Growth plc, which grows earnings regularly at a bit faster than the rate of inflation (say, at 8% per annum); and our friend above, Accelerated Earnings plc, which is expected to increase earnings by about 40% each year, at least in the next two years. Imagine also that they have all just reported earnings of £1m each. Then the analysts and the stock market might decide they are 'worthy' of the following PERs:

Slow Lane Industries plc PER	= 8 *times* earnings	= 8x
Modest Growth plc PER	= 12 *times* earnings	= 12x
Accelerated Earnings plc PER	= 30 *times* earnings	= 30x

Then the value of each of these firms in total would be

Slow Lane Industries plc – Value	= £1m x 8	= £8m
Modest Growth plc – Value	= £1m x 12	= £12m
Accelerated Earnings plc – Value	= £1m x 30	= £30m

In normal market conditions (that is, when the stock market is neither unusually high nor unusually low relative to normal valuations), the following rules of thumb apply in terms of PERs:

1. A PER of 5 or less means the stock market expects the company's earnings to decline severely, or thinks that the company may go bust.
2. A PER of 5–10 times means the stock market expects the company to grow its earnings at a rate slower than inflation (or for the earnings to decline).

3. A PER of 10–12 times means that earnings are expected to move roughly in line with inflation.
4. A PER of 12–15 means that earnings are expected to rise modestly ahead of inflation.
5. A PER of 15–20 times means that earnings are expected to increase well ahead of inflation.
6. A PER over 20 means that major earnings growth is anticipated.

MARKET VALUES, SHARE PRICES AND EARNINGS PER SHARE

One final word of explanation before moving on to how you can make money from this. We have talked thus far about the value of the total company. Unless you are fooling me, however, I don't think you intend to buy whole companies: you intend to buy shares. It is natural for people to focus, therefore, on the share price. But the right way to think about valuation is about what the total company is worth and what its earnings prospects are. You can then divide the total value by the number of shares to arrive at the share price.

✳ EXAMPLE Assume our favourite firm, Accelerated Earnings plc, had ten million shares. You remember that its total value is £30m, so the share price will be £30m divided by 1m, or £30 a share. You can apply this in reverse, if you know the share price and the number of shares, to calculate that Accelerated Earnings plc must have a market value of £30m. Then, if you knew the PER (for example by looking in the FT), and finding the PER is 30.0, then you could calculate that the firm's earnings must be £30m divided by 30, or £1m.

Next, you could also calculate the 'earnings per share' (EPS). If you knew that the total earnings were £1m and the number of shares one million, the earnings per share would be:

Earnings per share (EPS) = Total earnings *divided by* number of shares
= £1m *divided by* 1,000,000
= £1

Finally, if you knew the earnings per share and the share price, you could work out the PER for the company too:

Share price divided by earnings per share = PER
£30 *divided by* £1   = 30

SO WHAT?

The key points which you can use to make money are:

1. The PER determines the value of the company.
2. Selecting the PER (or deciding whether the current PER is appropriate) is very much an art, not a science.
3. The PER may change dramatically (up or down) if the expectation of future earnings changes considerably.
4. Changes in earnings growth have a disproportionate effect on the valuation of a company, because they affect both parts of the valuation equation (the earnings *and* the PER), and because therefore two higher (or lower) numbers are *multiplied* together.

Consider the following example.

Surprise Surprise plc produced earnings of £10m last year and is expected to produce the same again this year. It has a price earnings ratio of 10, which looks appropriate in the circumstances:

EXAMPLE ✳

Surprise Surprise plc – Earnings = £10m
Surprise Surprise plc – PER   = 10
Surprise Surprise plc – Value   = earnings *times* PER = £100m

All very boring. But now, Surprise Surprise plc lives up to its name and suddenly announces earnings of £15m, with a confident chairman's statement saying further earnings increases are on the way.

So earnings have gone up 50%, and the uninitiated (if delighted) shareholder might think that the most the shares can go up is 50%. But it's not just the earnings that change: their increase also leads the analysts to revise their views about Surprise Surprise plc and to say that a PER of 20 is now appropriate. So the earnings are up 50% and the PER has doubled. What does our bemused shareholder now expect: an increase in the value of his shares of between 50% and 100%? If so, he is in for another surprise:

Surprise Surprise plc – Earnings   = £15m
Surprise Surprise plc – PER   = 20
Surprise Surprise plc – Value   = £15m *times* 20 = £300m

In other words, the shares are now worth *three times* their previous value, even though earnings are only up 50%. There is a good reason for this because if earnings do continue to rise the cash which can be collected over the years goes up dramatically. Yet the effect in terms of share price appreciation can be stunning.

DOES RE-VALUATION OF A SHARE HAPPEN OVERNIGHT?

Only very rarely. You generally have to wait a few months or even a year or two before the market appreciates the change in trend and its implication for long-term valuation. This means that you cannot expect to see your shares triple over a week, though you may see this happen over a year or two, which should be good enough for most of us! *And herein lies your opportunity, not to be the lucky holder of shares with an earnings spurt, but to spot the earnings acceleration before the market marks up the shares appropriately.*

So at last (with apologies for the theoretical excursion into PERs) we reach the point of this chapter, and the basis for many investors' successful practice: buying shares in companies whose earnings are appreciating, before the PER adjusts as it should and probably will. This is a very exciting Way to beat the stock market, because it can produce a doubling or more in share values over a year or two, and it is eminently feasible for those who have the right skills and temperament.

HOW TO BACK THE HORSE AFTER THE WINNING POST

You might think that spotting earnings acceleration is a difficult or impossible task. The astonishing thing is that often all you need to do is to read

and interpret results that have already been published! In other words, you can sometimes back
the horse (buy the shares) after it has won the race
(raised earnings by a large percentage), but before
the share price has risen fully in response. This is
because the Price Earnings Ratio may not adjust

> **often all you need to do is to read and interpret results that have already been published!**

quickly or at all in the short run, but if and when it does, you could be
looking at a huge change in market value.

Filofax

EXAMPLE ✳

You might think this is too good to be true, but there are literally
hundreds of examples of cases where this has happened. The example of Filofax
has already been quoted (see pages 18–19). The interesting point is that even
after Filofax had turned in four half years of consistently growing earnings, and
after 1992/93 profits were 250% up on the year before, its share price was only
115p and its historic PER on 14 July 1993 was only 14.9 x, well below the market average at that time. If you had spotted the earnings acceleration earlier,
your shares would have increased from 40p to 115p, so you might be very
pleased.

But at the time, Filofax's stockbrokers, UBS, issued a research note forecasting
further growth in earnings (as, indeed, the company's annual report suggested).
The brokers estimated earnings of 10.0p in 1995. If that happened, and the
market generally continued to have an average PER of over 15, what value
might Filofax have? Clearly, the PER for an above average growth company
would be over 15, say 17.5 times earnings, which on 10p of earnings would give
a possible future value of 175p, or 52% above the price in July 1993.

By September 1993, the stock market had begun to notice the acceleration in
Filofax's earnings, and the shares reached 151p, up by 31% in two months. By
the time you read this you will know whether Filofax shares continued their
upward march, but there are only two possibilities: either the earnings growth
predicted will have come to pass, in which case the shares would have appreciated further; or the earnings growth will have failed to arrive.

➜ an update

The earnings growth continued and the shares continued to rise, reaching 277p by November 1995. In July, 1996, however, a profits warning knocked the shares back to 145p, before they began to recover again.

✳ EXAMPLE Pelican, 1992–93

Another example of rapid share price appreciation is the Pelican Group of restaurants in the last quarter of 1992 and the first three quarters of 1993. At the start of this period the shares were hovering in the low twenties (pence). At this time earnings growth was already apparent from the success of the Cafe Rouge chain, and analysts were projecting a rapid acceleration in profits that would put the shares on a ridiculously low price earnings ratio. The shares tripled within a year, as anticipated by several sources, including both the writer and the *Investors Chronicle* (see Figure IV.1).

✳ EXAMPLE Micro Focus

Another example of rapid share price appreciation, driven by accelerating earnings, is provided by Micro Focus during 1989, when the shares almost tripled (see Figure IV.2).

An interesting procedure is to index the share performance and also index on the same scale the reported operating profits, as shown in Figure IV.3. From this it can be seen that the share price began to move up in the month or so before announcement of the increase in profits, reflecting to some extent the analysts' forecasts would have justified a much larger increase than was actually forthcoming. When the results were announced, the shares did run up sharply, but again less than was justified by the increase in profits. This pattern was broadly repeated in the next period, where the shares gradually moved up to reflect recognition of the past earnings increase and to some extent anticipation of the next announcement. In the next period, the shares lagged behind what might have been expected from the earnings increase, until a spurt towards the end of 1989

The lesson is clear: there is often time to buy shares long after analysts are predicting earnings growth, and even after it has actually been announced, since it often takes time for the market to adjust to a company's status as a growth vehicle.

It is often very insightful to construct a chart similar to the one above for any share when earnings growth is happening. If the share price lags behind the profits growth it is a clear buy signal. Of course, this should not be read automatically: you should check if there is any good reason to expect the earnings surge to be temporary. Nevertheless, the chart is a good diagnostic device for predicting and monitoring share prices for growth companies.

Kwik Save

EXAMPLE ✳

Another illustration of this technique is provided by Kwik Save shares' behaviour between June 1988 and September 1989. As shown in Figure IV.4, the rapid growth in earnings announced initially had only a very mild positive effect on the share price. By the end of the succeeding six months, however, the share price had caught up with the previous percentage increase in profits, just in time to be met with another profit hike, which also had a delayed response in terms of share price appreciation. Thereafter, in the second half of 1989, the shares continued to rise, at last moving ahead of the percentage increase in profits, partly in anticipation of an increase in future earnings, and partly reflecting recognition that a higher price earnings ratio was justified.

WHY DO PER CHANGES LAG EARNINGS RISES?

It may seem surprising that you can 'back the horse after it passes the winning post'. There are three main reasons why this happens:

1. Careful analysis of the trend of earnings history is not yet well established in the UK. The focus of analysts is much more on the future than the past. Yet extrapolation of the past is a much more reliable guide to future share prices than the analysts' guesstimates of future earnings.

2. The market is often unduly sceptical about the sustainability of profit surges, and requires a long track record before it is willing to believe that the earnings will continue growing, or that they are high quality. Paradoxically, a company often reaches its peak PER *after* its period of maximum earnings growth. By then the period of maximum price appreciation is usually long past.

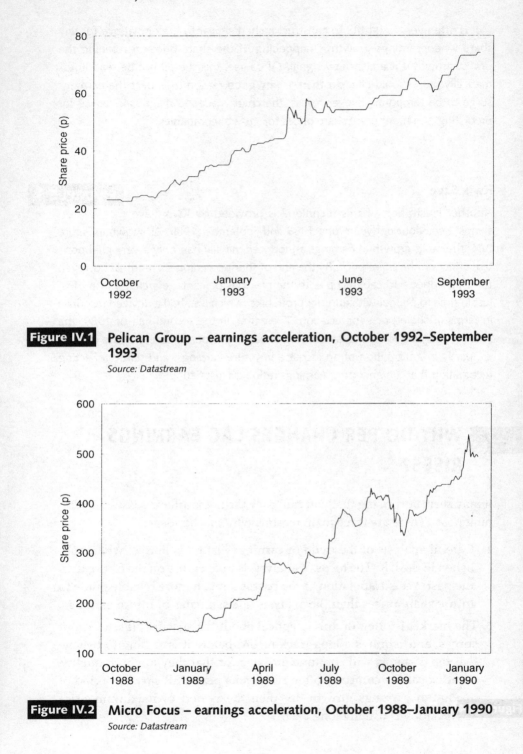

Figure IV.1 Pelican Group – earnings acceleration, October 1992–September 1993

Source: Datastream

Figure IV.2 Micro Focus – earnings acceleration, October 1988–January 1990

Source: Datastream

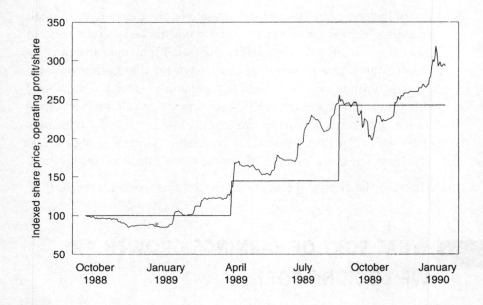

Figure IV.3 **Micro Focus – earnings acceleration, October 1988–January 1990**
Source: Company Accounts, Datastream, OC & C analysis

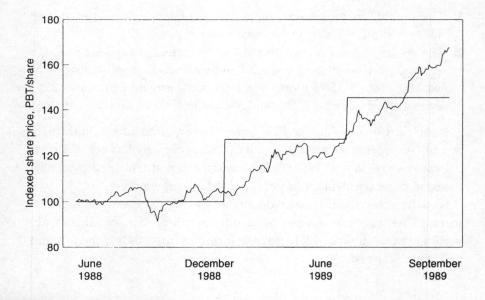

Figure IV.4 **Kwik Save – earnings acceleration, June 1988–September 1989**
Source: Datastream, OC & C analysis

3. Most of the companies that experience accelerating earnings are small or medium capitalisation stocks and are not tracked as fully (and in some cases scarcely at all) by quality analysts. Their small size can also reinforce the astute private investors' edge for three other reasons: some institutions may not invest in companies below a certain total value (but will when it crosses this boundary); private investors may find it easier to talk to smaller companies; and small companies may not be seen as quality investments (and hence worthy of high PERs) until they acquire a certain amount of publicity and recognition.

But whatever the causes, the key is to exploit this market imperfection!

WHAT SORT OF EARNINGS GROWTH ARE WE LOOKING FOR?

Well, we are *not* talking about acceleration of earnings growth from 5% per annum to 10% per annum, even though this is a doubling and certainly counts as 'acceleration'. I suggest two conditions both have to be fulfilled:

1. The annual (or annualised) rate of growth of earnings must be at least 30% per annum. This is the *minimum level of growth*.
2. The annualised *rate* of growth must be an increase of at least 50%. For example, if the earnings growth before was 20%, it must now be at least 30% (that is, 50% more than 20%); if the growth before was 25%, it must now be at least 37 5%, and so on. *This is the acceleration condition*.

A significant increase in the PER cannot be expected unless both these conditions are met, but if they are, it can. If a company has been increasing earnings steadily at 10% per annum and this suddenly spurts to 40%, the conditions are ideal for future rapid share price increases.

Now let's talk about how to identify and verify these desirable investments. There are three stages: (a) identifying prima facie candidates; (b) verifying the history; and (c) assessing future prospects. Only then should you actually invest.

IDENTIFYING PRIME FACIE 'ACCELERATORS'

First, catch your fish. Before you can analyse candidates that you think may be an 'accelerator' (my shorthand for a company that fulfils the growth and acceleration conditions laid out above), you first need to identify them.

The best sources for this are the financial press, plus any stockbrokers' literature you may receive. If you are serious about this Way, you should read the financial pages of a quality daily, and look out for any announcements of annual or half yearly earnings surges. Remember that the best candidates are generally those neglected by others, so look for small headlines or the one or two line digests often accorded to smaller companies. A very useful supplement is the summary of results each week in the *Investors Chronicle*, which gives the percentage annual change. Serious investors may also wish to subscribe to *The Estimates Directory*, which summarises brokers' forecasts for most quoted companies.

> **Remember that the best candidates are generally those neglected by others.**

You may supplement this, of course, with news of companies you know, or direct observation of companies that appear to be growing fast (for example, a retailer opening new stores at a fast rate, or a manufacturer whose product everyone suddenly seems to be using), where you may suspect there is earnings growth even before you look at the numbers.

When you have a shortlist of candidates, or in exceptional cases just one, it is time to start analysing. It is generally better to look at a handful of candidates together, so that you can rank their relative attractiveness and avoid putting a positive construction on one possibility simply because it is your only available choice.

VERIFYING THE HISTORY

Now comes the analytical bit. Although the concepts and analysis are quite straightforward, you will require a degree of numeracy and confidence in dealing with the profit and loss statement to undertake this. If you find yourself lost or confused in what follows, you must either find a more experienced friend who is willing and able to do the analysis for you, or else you should select another Way to superior performance! You will need some hints now as to how to proceed with your analysis.

1. Which profits to look at?

We have talked thus far about after tax profits or earnings, as these are the basis of price earnings multiples and company valuations. Yet sometimes the underlying rate of growth of a company is distorted if you look just at earnings, because of a sudden (but not sustainable) change in the tax rate. The best measure of underlying growth is Profit Before Interest and Taxes, usually called Operating Profit. If this is not available in the half yearly results, use Profit Before Tax instead. You should therefore apply the two tests above (of Earnings Growth and Earnings Acceleration) to Operating Profits (or Profit Before Tax), and reject any company that does not pass these tests.

> **You should certainly reject any company where earnings per share is not positive.**

On the other hand, you should beware of a situation in which Operating Profit grows rapidly, perhaps by acquisition, but the number of shares in existence goes up rapidly too. So you should also look at the change in earnings per share (EPS), and look closely at any company where this does not also meet the above tests.

You should certainly reject any company where earnings per share is not positive, but if the difference between the Operating Profit growth and the EPS growth is accounted for solely by a one-time change in the tax rate, you may feel that the Operating Profit is the more important guide.

✳ EXAMPLE Manchester Metro plc makes an Operating Profit and Profit Before Tax in 1997 of £100m, but because it has a lot of tax losses available, pays only a 10% tax rate and makes £90m after tax. In 1998 Operating Profit and Profit Before Tax jumps to £150m but the venture now pays a full 35% tax rate, so the earnings only rise to £97.5m. The two profit measures therefore show very different growth rates:

	1996	1997
Operating profit (& PBT)	£100m	£150m
Tax rate	10%	35%
Earnings	£90m	£97.5m

– Operating Profit (& PBT) growth		50%
– Earnings and EPS growth		8.3%

Which is the better guide to future growth? If the tax rate stays at 35%, probably the Operating Profit, as the following numbers (also invented) show:

	1996	1997	1998
Operating profit (& PBT)	£100m	£150m	£210m
Tax rate	10%	35%	35%
Earnings	£90m	£97.5m	£136.5m
– Operating Profit		50%	40%
– Earnings and EPS		8.3%	40%

2. Over what time period?

In the UK all quoted companies give half yearly profits (a few larger ones, with which we are probably not concerned here, give quarterly profits). The question is, how can you be confident that the earnings growth is not just a one-off, never to be repeated, surge? You can never be totally sure, but there are some guidelines:

(a) **Look at the earnings over the past six, eight or ten half-year periods.** Then look at the percentage changes in Operating Profit and earnings per share. What you want to see is a flattish profits in the first periods followed by a steady but increasing acceleration in the growth rates, with no sign yet that the rate of increase is dropping off:

A desirable pattern

	P1	P2	P3	P4	P5	P6
Earnings	100	105	112	130	160	253
% increase		5	7	16	30	50

What you do not want to see are volatile earnings with a history of ups and downs, even if the recent trend is up:

An undesirable pattern

	P1	P2	P3	P4	P5	P6
Earnings	100	130	105	95	140	180
% increase		30	−19	−10	47	29

(b) Correct for seasonality. Many companies (for instance retailers) have highly seasonal businesses, so that they make most of their money in the second half, which includes Christmas. You should therefore compare the relevant half years:

Seasonal business desirable profit pattern

Year	First half	Second half	Total
1989	20	80	100
1990	20	90	110
1991	25	130	155
1992	37	208	245
1993	65	420	485

Note that the percent increases in the above table look unattractive if you do not adjust for seasonality, but if you compare the half-year results with the equivalent previous half year, the percentage increases run as follows, showing a good run up:

0% (first half of 1990 versus first half of 1989), 12.5% (second half of 1990 versus second half of 1989), 25%, 44%, 48%, 60%, 76%, 102%. In this case the annual figures would provide a good guide, but you should always use the latest available half-yearly data, and compare it to earlier relevant half-years.

3. Eliminate historical exceptional distortions

Look out for distortions in earnings because of extraordinary gains or losses. These have now been eliminated by the adoption of a new accounting rule (FRS 3), but you should look out for historical distortions.

ASSESSING FUTURE PROFIT TRENDS

There are four ways in which you can assess the future profit trends. At least three of these indicators should be highly positive for you to go ahead and buy shares.

1. Extrapolation

The point of conducting the above analyses is to see what the long-term trend is. In my experience, percentage extrapolation is often a more reliable indicator of the future (certainly the medium to long term) than the careful calculations of experts.

When you extrapolate, look at the trend and at the rate of change. If you have access to 'semi-log' paper, use that to extrapolate earnings. If not, look at the percentage changes and see whether the rate of change is increasing or decreasing before making your extrapolation. Even if the numbers are going up, the *rate* of increase may be falling, as in the series 5, 10, 15, 20, 25. Always check whether the percentage increase is rising or falling.

2. The company's own comments

These will come in announcements with the results, which will then be incorporated in the annual or interim reports, and may also come in periodic announcements to the stock markets.

You will need to read the financial press for the latter, but annual reports can be obtained free of charge by telephoning or writing to the company secretary of your potential investment. Be sure to specify precisely the reports you want (e.g. the annual report plus interim reports for 1990–93) and ask to be put on the mailing list for future reports. In some cases they may not have spare copies of some older reports and you may have to go to a business library to check these.

Read the words carefully and see how far the company has identified the causes of its growth and how far it thinks they can be extended or sustained.

You may rightly object that company chairmen have differing personalities, degrees of optimism or caution in what they say. Precisely! The great thing is that (unless the chairman is new and has never held a similar post before) you can check his or her track record. Look at what he or she has said before and how far you would have over- or under-estimated the next year's results based on his comments. Only then can you decode the message to you today.

3. Analysts' projections

If you are thinking of buying shares in a company you should read at least one of the current reports from analysts, particularly from those who are also the stockbrokers to the company. Your stockbroker should be able to send you one or more of these reports.

4. Your own investigations and synthesis

Remember that if a company's earnings are surging and due to continue doing so, *there must be a reason in the real world.* You must be happy in your own mind that you have identified the main cause or causes of the profit growth. Having done so, you must reach a view, if necessary by conducting your own primary investigation, as to whether and for how long the growth is likely to continue. If you conclude that the earnings jump has been based at least 50% on luck or on one-off events, do not invest.

▮ THE INVESTMENT DECISION CHECKLIST

Now is the time to decide whether to invest in each of your candidates. The following checklist has been designed to allow you to measure their relative and absolute attractiveness. Go through and mark each company and then compare the scores.

1. *How much has operating profit in the last two sixth-month periods gone up? (Remember to compare each half to the same half a year earlier if it is a seasonal business.)*

   a. by an annual rate of 20% or less in each period   (score 0)

   b. by an annual rate of between 21% and 30% in each period (score 10)

   c. by an annual rate of between 31% and 40% in each period (score 15)

   d. by an annual rate of over 40% in each period   (score 20)

   e. by an annual rate of less than 20% in the penultimate period but 21–30% in the last period   (score 5)

f. by an annual rate of 21–30% in the penultimate period but by 31–40% in the last period   (score 15)

g. by an annual rate of 31–40% in the penultimate period but by over 40% in the last period   (score 20)

h. by less than 20% in the penultimate period but over 30% in the last period   (score 10)

2. *What does the pattern of operating profit growth look like in the last 6–10 half-year periods?*

a. no clear growth trend   (score 0)

b. growth trend but with some volatility and reversals   (score 5)

c. clear growth trend, but growth is not currently accelerating (score 15)

d. consistent and accelerating growth trend   (score 25)

3. *Has earnings per share history broadly been similar to the operating profit history above?*

a. yes   (no points)

b. no, because of changes in the tax rate, but otherwise yes   (no points)

c. no, because there have been new shares issued   (In this case, look at the approximate percentage EPS growth compared to Operating Profit growth, and scale down the score you have so far given accordingly. For example, if Operating Profit growth was over 40%, but EPS growth only 20%, your score of 20 under (d) above should be reduced to 10.)

4. *Based on the your best guess at extrapolating the past numbers, would you expect annual earnings growth in the next 2–3 years to average:*

a. less than 20%?   (no points)

b. 20–29%?   (10 points)

c. 30–39%?   (15 points)

d. 40–49%?   (20 points)

    e. 50–75%?   (30 points)

    f. over 75%?   (50 points)

5. *Repeat question 4, but this time for the analysts' projections of the growth rates. Award the same points as for the scoring system in (4) above.*

6. *If you had to interpret the chairman's and other company statements alone and guess the future annual growth rate in earnings from that, taking into account the previous accuracy or otherwise of his or her projections, would your best guess be:*

    a. under 20%?   (no points)

    b. 20–39%?   (10 points)

    c. 40–75%?   (20 points)

    d. over 75%?   (30 points)

7. *Do you believe you understand the 'real world' reasons for the profit surge?*

    a. yes, and it is probably sustainable over the next 2–3 years   (30 points)

    b. any other answer   (no points)

Now add up the total number of points you have accumulated. If the number is 50 or fewer, reject the candidate. If the number is 55 or more, then divide this number by the historic PER of the company.

Example: Your total score is 75. The PER is 15.

       Company attractiveness = 75 divided by 15 = 5

Interpreting the Investment Decision Checklist Score

Less than 3 **Do not invest**

3.0 to 3.9 **Moderately attractive:** try to find better candidates

4.0 to 4.9 **Attractive**

5.0 to 5.9 **Very attractive:** potential to double your money within two years if you are right

6.0 to 10 **Exceptionally attractive:** definite potential to multiply your investment if you are right

Over 10 Check your calculations. Then check your numbers. Get a friend to re-check everything. Then if it still scores over 10, make this your biggest single investment!

MULTIPLYING YOUR MONEY

Earlier in the chapter we gave many real-life examples where shares had more than doubled within three years because of earnings growth and upward revision of PERs. But it is instructive to see how this works using a hypothetical candidate you may have evaluated in the above manner. You can then adapt the worked example to your top candidate to see what sort of gain you might expect if you are right about the future earnings growth.

Let us assume that an entrepreneur has set up Value Exchange, a chain of bureaux de changes in UK tourist centres. This is different **EXAMPLE ✳** from all other such bureaux in that it really does offer good value for money, charging no commission and yet offering a competitive rate of exchange, so that its 'take' is on average half that of competitors. The chain is aggressively promoted in tourist publications and by local advertising. Although its margins are much thinner than average, it soon attracts an enormous amount of business, which is also boosted by its policy of offering free coffee to the queues that rapidly develop.

Value Exchange plc has a three-year trading record of growth in revenues and profits of 50% per annum and goes public forecasting earnings for 1993 of £5m. The company is valued on flotation on a modest prospective PER of 12.

You conduct your research while waiting to see if the profit forecast is realised. In fact, Value Exchange plc makes profit after tax of £5.5m in 1993, beating its forecast. Meanwhile you discover that Value Exchange has a plan to open similar outlets in British tourist centres abroad, starting with Spain. You reckon that if all goes according to plan – and the management seems competent – earnings in the UK alone will guarantee minimum annual profit growth of 30%, and this could be over 40% if the Spanish initiative is successful.

You put Value Exchange through the Investment Decision Checklist mincer, and it scores a conservative 100 points on questions 1–7. Meanwhile you are disappointed to find out that its share price has gone up 37.5% since flotation. It is now on a historic PER of 15 based on profits of £5.5m, and its total market value is now therefore £5.5m x 15 = £82.5m, compared to £60m (£5m x 12) on flotation. You wonder whether you might have missed the boat!

Yet when you divide the 100 points by the new historic PER of 15, you still arrive at a score of 6.7, which according to the table above is 'exceptionally attractive'. You buy the shares at 137.5p (they floated at 100p).

The profits do work out pretty much as you expected! In 1994 earnings are up 30% (the Spanish plans have been delayed by bureaucracy out there), and in 1995 the benefits of Spain start to show through, with earnings up 45% to £10.4m. Now people have started to believe in the future overseas potential, there is a general expectation that Value Exchange plc will produce earnings growth of over 30% for the next few years, and the PER has gone up to 25 times earnings.

What are your shares worth? A simple calculation shows the value of the total company now is:

$$\text{Value of Value Exchange plc} = \text{Earnings } \textit{times} \text{ PER}$$
$$= £10.4\text{m} \times 22.5$$
$$= £234\text{m}$$

This £234m compares with £82.5m when you started two years ago, an increase of 184%! In other words you have nearly tripled your money, with the share price now at 390p.

Interestingly, if you now re-applied the Investment Decision Checklist, Value Exchange plc would now score about 80 (lower than the original 100, because the expected future growth rate is now a bit lower) divided by the new PER of 22.5, for a net score of 3.55, rated above as 'moderately attractive'. You would probably still get a return well above average for the market from Value Exchange plc, provided things ran according to plan, but the period of dramatic gains is probably over, because the PER has gone up already and is unlikely to go much higher. You should be able to find better opportunities elsewhere.

PREDICTING PROFIT GROWTH BEFORE IT MATERIALISES

Our focus so far has been spotting profit growth which has already been reported but not fully reflected in the market price. But you should keep your eyes open for cases where there is a real surge in activity and potentially in profits, but before these profits have yet been earned or reported. If you can spot a profit surge before it happens, you can make even greater returns than those illustrated above. Remember that in many cases when a company expands there are start-up costs and necessary investments before profits can show through. An increase in turnover and market share is often a leading indicator for profit growth.

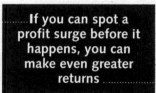

If you can spot a profit surge before it happens, you can make even greater returns

As you look about you, remember the main real world reasons why companies can suddenly produce a spurt in earnings:

1. Extension of a proven product or service into a new geographical region (at home or overseas: but remember the additional risk with the latter).
2. A distinctly superior new product or service that is gaining market share hand over fist.
3. A new product or service that is proving successful in early tests.
4. The ability to put prices up, because there is no consumer resistance or competition (interestingly, this sometimes happens when commodity prices like tea or coffee advance, and consumers expect a similar increase in the price in the supermarkets, although the actual raw material cost may be a small part of the total).
5. A dramatic reduction in the cost base (it is intriguing that shares often decline on news of major redundancies, presumably because the market thinks these are a reaction to hard times rather than a proactive attempt to widen margins).

It is now time to sum up the pros and cons of this Way.

✔ Advantages... *of detecting earnings acceleration*

1. This Way offers the prospect for really high capital growth, while not necessarily being speculative or even very risky. The degree of risk can be assessed and reduced by careful research before making the investment.

2. The Way exploits two real market imperfections that lead the stock market to undervalue high growth companies in the early stages of the growth. These imperfections are: the crude way in which PERs are assessed; and the lack of confidence in the sustainability of early earnings growth, where with good homework you can hope to know more than the market as a whole about the company concerned.

3. The method above, and in particular the Investment Decision Checklist, enables you to rank and compare a number of prospective investments.

4. The calculation of potential future earnings and PERs enables you to guess where the share price might go. Seeing this happen in practice can be great fun (although not seeing it happen is less fun).

✗ Disadvantages... *of detecting earnings acceleration*

1. To do this properly requires numeracy, a degree of investigation, and quite a lot of analysis. In short, it can be pretty hard work. You should only follow this method if you enjoy pursuing it: otherwise it will be a burden and probably done badly.

2. It takes time.

3. Those who are swayed too much by hope and too little by analysis can find this a dangerous method. If you have poor judgment you will make bad investments.

4. This Way tends to be biased towards smaller companies, and therefore the risk is likely to be higher than average.

WHO IS THIS WAY BEST FOR?

This is an analytical Way par excellence. It requires a fair amount of skill in dealing with numbers (though this should not be exaggerated) and quite a lot of patience. It requires a time horizon of at least 2–3 years per investment, but not necessarily a very long horizon. It is suitable for our personality Types 2 and 3, but generally not for Type 1 (who may wear rose-tinted spectacles).

➤ Overall evaluation

This is a proven way of beating the market when operated well. It can offer exceptional returns, although with above average risk. The risks can be reduced by prior analysis and investigation, but not removed. More than most, this Way is one which either appeals to you as an individual, or it does not. If you like it and have the skills required, it is highly recommended.

WAY V

Outsider information

This way suits risk-taking extroverts with plenty of time and enthusiasm for their investment activities.

WHAT IS OUTSIDER INFORMATION?

'Outsider information' is information gathered on a company by outside research which can be used to inform share purchase or sale decisions. 'Insider information' is used for the same purpose, but outsider information is different in a number of ways:

1. Outsider information is not short-term, price-sensitive information obtained from a contact inside the company. Instead, it is your own market research from talking to a variety of sources including customers, competitors, and suppliers of the company in question as well as industry observers and other outside experts. Outsider information can also include data gleaned from talking to employees of the company, provided they are told honestly that you are a researcher or investor and do not divulge information of a price sensitive nature.
2. Outsider information is concerned with the long-term market and competitive position of the company, not with short-term 'secrets' regarding impending actions or deals.
3. Outsider information requires data gathering, analysis and reflection before making purchase or sale decisions.
4. Outsider information, correctly analysed, is much more reliable than insider information, where the rumoured deal may never happen or the market reaction may be different from what was expected.
5. Most importantly, use of outsider information is completely legal, whereas insider information can land you inside one of HM Prisons.

WHY DOES OUTSIDER INFORMATION MAKE SENSE?

It's a curious thing, but it is often easier for an intelligent and well-informed outsider to see what is going on in an industry or among a group of competitors than it is for either those inside the company, or stock market analysts, to do the same. The company person usually has a distorted view of the Universe, thinking that the Sun revolves around his or her own company, and is often blinded by the company's ideology or way of doing things. The company person may well miss what competitors are doing, even when it is obvious to outsiders. For example, the management of Filofax in 1989–90 saw sales declining and assumed that, with the 'death of the Yuppie', their market was disappearing, whereas the truth was that Filofax at that time was losing massive market share to cheaper competitors, while the market itself continued to grow.

> .... One of the most important keys is what customers think of particular products and companies. ....

The stockbrokers' analyst has a different problem. Most of the information looked at is narrowly financial, or general information gathered from the company itself. True, the analyst will visit several different companies in the industry, but the focus will generally be short term, trying to guess profit outcomes rather than thinking about what will determine those profits in the medium and long term. You can and should use stockbrokers' reports, but you can supplement these with your own judgment.

Someone with the right temperament, training and time can actually do a better job of researching what is going on, and spot trends that will eventually have really major effects, on the value of a company. One of the most important keys is what customers think of particular products and companies. Published market research is usually too general and unfocused to help here. Your own market research can be the best guide.

THREE COMPONENTS OF OUTSIDER INFORMATION

There are three different elements here, all of which should be used, though you may enjoy and be best at one of the three, and can concentrate your energies there:

1. The opinion gathering/journalistic approach.
2. The management/employee assessment approach.
3. Micro-economic/competitive analysis.

The journalistic approach

Many astute investors are like good journalists or detectives. Some people are under the impression that these two professions tend to swan around, gossiping and drinking until something interesting turns up. Actually, good journalists and detectives are very focused in terms of what they want to find out, although they are open to any unanticipated inputs which help reveal the answer.

> ..... **At its simplest, you may spot a product or service which seems to be taking off.** ....

For you as an investor, to make investigation worthwhile, you must have an idea to test, a hypothesis to prove or disprove, that could have a major impact on a company's long-term fortunes. It could be a very simple idea, an instinct, which you do not yet know is correct, but which, if correct, could have major implications.

At its simplest, you may spot a product or service which seems to be taking off. A retailer or restaurant may be opening lots of new outlets (which is interesting these days because it is unusual), or you may notice that a lot more shelf space is being allocated to a new product, or all your business friends may be talking about a new computer or software package. In terms of making money from shares, this would be of absolutely no interest if the company concerned was not a quoted public company or if the product or service made up just a small share of its total sales.

But assume that you have found such a product or service – what next?

You notice that Cafe Rouge restaurants are springing up every- **EXAMPLE ✻** where. You find out that they are owned by a company called Pelican, which owns two Pelican brasseries in London, but whose fortunes are now largely influenced by the Cafe Rouge chain. You then want to talk to anyone who might tell you how good the formula is and what the scope for expansion is, and how much money is being made.

As a good journalist/detective, you will talk to people in the restaurants or coming out of them, to find out how highly they rated what our American friends direly call the 'eating experience'; you will talk to your friends or to a group of the target population (people in their twenties and thirties) to find out if they have heard of Cafe Rouge, and if so what they think of it; you will find a few industry experts who will tell you what is going on; you will talk to a few of the staff to find out whether they like working there and what their view of the company is; and so on.

The root cause of a company's expansion is always that it is doing something better or different that customers like. Someone with the right mentality, who is open to new information, can hope to see this before others. The key point, though, is not just to detect a trend, but to be sure that the customers feel very strongly in favour of the product or service. If this is true, even in a local area, the company will eventually overcome distribution barriers and be able to become very much bigger.

The management/employee assessment approach

A simple test is to divide companies into the 'sheep' and the 'goats' based on how enthusiastic people in the company are about it. Walk into most companies, and you get the impression that people are just doing a job, conscientiously perhaps, but without real enthusiasm. Go into some other companies, however, and you are struck by a sense of vitality and purpose, momentum and team work, and the thought strikes you: people like working here, believe in the company, and actually want to reach out and help customers. The receptionist is happy and welcoming. People are zooming about, intent on some mission or other. There are clusters of people talking and laughing, but then dashing off to get on with their work.

This latter group are the companies in which you ought to invest. If you have contact with a company, it is remarkably easy to spot the companies where people believe in what they are doing, where they bubble over with enthusiasm. Go and see.

Next, go and talk to the people running the company, and look for the same sort of dedication and fanaticism. They should eat, drink and sleep their company. They should be open-minded, determined to expand, and receptive to customer feedback. These things can be assessed by anyone talking to them, and are far more important in most companies than technical skill (which is also more difficult to assess).

Then visit the firm's main competitors. If they are equally gung-ho, or almost so, this does not give you a clear investment signal. What you want to find is that the competitors are arrogant, complacent, defensive, unenthusiastic and generally down in the dumps: then the first company, with its winning culture, should make mincemeat of the competitors sooner or later, and you do have a definite green light for share purchase.

Micro-economic/competitive analysis

The third and final approach to outsider information is to gather information on the competitive position of your target company and conduct analysis of this. Whole books have been written on this subject and it is not easy to learn to do this from scratch, but the essential points can be summarised quite shortly.

The micro-economic approach says: look what is happening when companies collide and compete with one another. In some markets, there is not much change in the share of the market which different companies have. Pepsi Cola and Coca-Cola tend to have the same market shares and

> the micro-economist will look at the potential, and buy the shares.

these do not change much in most countries. But in other markets, the share that different companies have can change, gradually or suddenly, and this can make a huge difference over ten years.

It follows that the best indicator of long-term profits is the trend in market share. Now, the interesting thing is that although a company may already be gaining market share, this may not yet show up (or show up fully) in its short-term financial results. Although the sales will be increasing, the profits may not go up at anything like this rate, or may actually go down. This is because gaining market share may require investment: in a new factory, in hiring more salespeople, in advertising, or in lowering prices. The stock market will look at the near-term profit trend, and not be impressed. But the micro-economist will look at the potential, and buy the shares.

There are many examples where this approach has worked. At the level of a whole industry or indeed country, look at Japan. Honda and Yamaha took on the British motor-cycle industry in the 1960s and 1970s and virtually wiped the latter out. Anyone who had spotted the market share trend in the 1960s could easily have predicted what actually happened, and sold shares in the British companies before they became worthless. The same applies to personal computers, where Apple and others have put increasing pressure on IBM, or to photocopiers, where Xerox lost share to Japanese producers like Ricoh, Canon and Mitsubishi slowly but surely over three decades.

As before, you should be looking for situations which are 'make or break' as far as the company is concerned, and you should be looking at long-term trends. This approach is different from the two above, however, in that it generally relies on published information to a much greater extent, and requires skill in analysis and interpretation of the data so that you do not make wrong assumptions.

LEONARD COHEN'S WILD JOKER

One of Leonard Cohen's songs includes a line about finding 'a card so high and wild, you'll never need to find another'. This is intriguing advice for the practitioner of outsider information. For this approach is time-consuming and hard work, if followed at all diligently, and it requires a few major discoveries to make it all worthwhile.

If you do uncover a share which is already gaining market share steadily and has terrific growth potential not yet recognised by the stock market, you should be sure to make a significant investment. This does present a problem if you believe in diversifying away risk. My advice here is half way between the Leonard Cohen and the risk averse diversifier. I suggest putting up to 25% of your available funds into your 'discovery', but making sure that the remaining 75% is spread between about ten shares. But then don't worry if your Wild Joker goes up in value and starts to constitute a major part of your portfolio. Don't sell too early, or at all, while the company continues to gain market share, or until the market realises the eventual financial implications.

> Don't worry if your Wild Joker goes up in value and starts to constitute a major part of your portfolio.

Advantages... *of outsider information*

1. This Way offers a real prospect of finding companies with unappreciated, long-term economic value. If you are good at a combination of the three approaches above, you should find a few gems.
2. You only need a few such winners, held over a long time, to make money out of this Way.
3. If you have the right temperament and enjoy meeting people, this can become an enjoyable hobby as well as being profitable.

✗ Disadvantages... *of outsider information*

1. The up-front time and effort required is considerable. This is not arm-chair investing.
2. It requires skill and tenacity, as well as self-confidence to back your judgment, when few if any stock market experts will be drawing attention to your selections. If you lack these traits, you will be miserable and anxious, and should not take this on.
3. You are likely to end up with a lop-sided portfolio, heavily concentrated in a few stocks or with one being dominant in terms of value. Inevitably, this brings above average risk.
4. The risk element may also be greater because this Way tends to be skewed towards investment in smaller companies. This is not necessarily true, as some of the examples of big companies gaining share for decades illustrates, but most outsider information devotees do end up outside blue-chip shares.
5. It can take a while before the causes of superior performance (like market share gain) work through to produce marked share price appreciation. This Way is therefore not recommended for short-term investors or those who may need to 'go liquid' at short notice.

WHO IS THIS WAY BEST FOR?

The short answer is, anyone who enjoys it! Some analytical skill is required, but the key things are to work out what you want to find out, to enjoy talking and listening to others, to have good judgment and the confidence to back it.

This Way is most likely to fit Type 1 or 2 personalities. If you are that rare breed, the extrovert analyst, you will probably enjoy this method. Short-term or nervous investors should steer clear of this Way.

► Overall evaluation

This Way offers a real prospect of identifying long-term value not yet evident in profits or share prices. It requires energy and enterprise. If you have the right personality and skills, a long time horizon, and do not mind taking some risk, this Way should serve you well.

Good businesses

This Way requires energy, knowledge of basic accounting and a long time horizon. It can be very attractive to Type 2 personalities.

WARREN BUFFETT'S BIG IDEA

Investment maestro Warren Buffett has declared that there is no need for investors to come up with lots of new ideas. A few, or even one, may be much better. Buffett himself had one 'big idea': that American local newspapers, where they had a monopoly, constituted the most perfect business franchise. This simple idea has made him a fortune.

More broadly, as a great simplifier, Buffett divides businesses into 'good' and 'bad', the sheep and the goats. This is the investment equivalent of Calvinism, a belief in Original Sin, that some businesses are damned to poor profitability and best avoided, a salutary correction to the mindless optimism that all businesses can be turned around by the injection of great managers. Though examples can be touted where apparently hopeless businesses have been turned around, Buffett's approach of investing only in businesses which are clearly 'good' has much to commend it: it avoids unnecessary risk, and has produced excellent returns as well.

> Buffett's approach of investing only in businesses which are clearly 'good' has much to commend it.

GOOD BUSINESSES

A good business is not necessarily a 'blue chip' or big business. It can be quite small, and need not be very old. Sometimes entrepreneurs may spot a potential niche for a good business that does not yet exist, and build it up very quickly. My definition of a good business is one that has a high return on capital, defensible competitive advantage, and a sharp, winning culture. You might think that good businesses are always expensive, but you would be wrong. Sometimes good businesses are as cheap as bad (or less good) businesses, and quite frequently good businesses are only a little more expensive than non-good businesses. Yet good businesses will always produce a high return for the long-term investor.

Why does this market imperfection exist? One key reason is that few investors have really appreciated the power of the simple concept of 'good' businesses. Another key reason is that it is not always easy to decide what is really a good business, as opposed to one that just looks good now, but lacks true quality. Before long I will give some hints on how to identify good businesses and test whether a candidate really is 'good', but first it may help to give some examples.

GOOD BUSINESSES THAT PAID OFF FOR BUFFETT

First, some American examples of good companies invested in by Warren Buffett. Between 1973 and 1985 Buffett built up a holding in Affiliated Publications, a media company with the sort of local monopoly beloved by Buffett. The company owns *The Boston Globe*, which is the largest newspaper in New England, as well as having interests in cable TV and radio. Buffett's holding cost $3.5m and he sold it in 1986 for $75m.

Buffett also invested in 1973 in the Washington Post Company. In 1985 he sold part of his holding at a profit of 1,868%. Since then the company has continued to perform well above the market average.

Buffett tripled his money by buying shares in Time Inc. (publisher of *Time*, *Fortune* and other leading magazines) between 1982 and 1985, selling out in 1986.

Another Buffett coup was in Interpublic Group, which, in the 1980s, was the largest advertising agency system in the world. Buffett was one of the first people to recognise the potential of advertising agencies to gain a global franchise, so that multinational companies would have little choice as to whom to use for their campaigns. He also sold out before the delusions of grandeur induced by success could wreak their havoc: but he was scarcely a short-term investor even here. He began to buy Interpublic in 1973 and by the end of 1982 had paid $4.5m for his stake. Between 1983 and 1985 he sold 55% of his shares for no less than $26.4m. He made similar returns in another agency, Ogilvy & Mather, which was bought at the top of the cycle by Martin Sorrell's WPP.

Not all of Buffett's 'good businesses' were in media. In 1981–83 he bought into General Foods, the owner of Maxwell House and a clutch of other leading American branded foodstuffs. In 1985 Philip Morris acquired General Foods and Buffett collected a return on his shares of 238%.

BRITISH EXAMPLES OF GOOD BUSINESSES

I have selected a few examples of British companies which pass my tests (given below) of 'good businesses'. These companies have all out-performed the stock market over long periods of time (and may well be expected to do so in the future). This helps to illustrate the point that, like some alien humanoid clothed in our flesh and walking the earth undetected, 'good' companies go about their business in a way that leaves them unnoticed by most observers and investors. They sell at little more in terms of price earnings ratios than their 'non-good' counterparts and yet produce returns over decades that surpass the average. This is because, being 'good', they are able to grow their profits at a rate which is both faster than the average, and faster than the analysts at any given time are likely to expect.

Shell

EXAMPLE ✳

Shell has high market shares in all of its most important markets and at each stage of the exploration/production/marketing value added chain. It has been financially strong for generations and is hugely cash generative. It has a cult of technical competence, and although somewhat bureaucratic, it is redeemed by its professionalism. It has used its market power wisely and unobtrusively and cultivated effective alliances with governments of whatever complexion. It has a great brand and strong customer appreciation.

From an investment viewpoint, the old marketing slogan, 'You Can Be Sure of Shell', applies nicely. Shell will rarely top the investment charts, but can generally be relied upon to turn in a solid and above average performance. Figure VI.1 shows an annual growth rate since 1975 of 21% in Shell's share price.

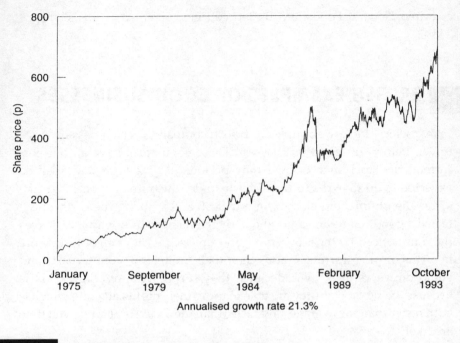

Annualised growth rate 21.3%

Figure VI.1 **Shell, January 1975–October 1993**
Source: Datastream

✳ EXAMPLE **Cadbury Schweppes**

Cadbury Schweppes has high market shares in the chocolate confectionery business in most of its key countries: the market has high barriers to entry and is usually dominated by three players. It has a great brand name and good nice positions in soft drinks too. Strong brands, excellent marketing, impressive cash generation, and a self-confident culture combined with commercial realism, characterise the company. Cadbury also has the attraction that it is one of the very few viable acquisition candidates worldwide in its industries: acquisition would be expensive, but is not impossible to imagine.

These reasons would lead one to expect above average investment performance over long periods of time. This is indeed the case. From 1975 to 1993 Cadbury Schweppes shares grew at an annual rate of almost 19% compounded (see Figure VI.2). Cadbury Schweppes is another in the Shell category of solid, above average performers.

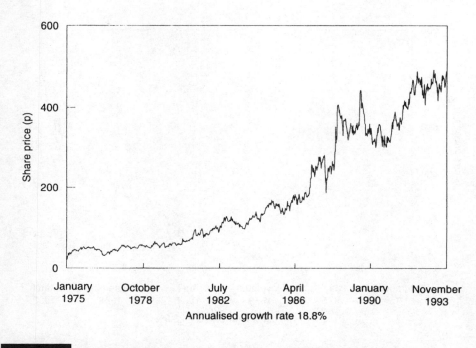

Figure VI.2 **Cadbury Schweppes, January 1975–November 1993**
Source: Datastream

Not all good businesses have excellent brands of premium positioning.
Kwik Save is an example of a good business that is a market leader, but in
the no-frills grocery retailing arena.

Kwik Save

EXAMPLE ✳

Kwik Save is a 'formula business', that has discovered discount retailing and built
up appropriate skills and systems. It too has attractive cash characteristics and
good management.

Kwik Save has a very impressive record of growth in profits and share price.
From 1971 to the spring of 1993, the compound annual growth in share price
was nearly 24% (see Figure VI.3).

Recently, the group has been affected by concerns about the retail sector, particularly the potential growth of deep discounters and warehouse clubs at the expense
of more conventional supermarkets. Kwik Save's rating has been affected, even
though analysts are predicting further share growth in the next two years. We will
see whether Kwik Save continues to be a good business from an investment perspective. I, for one, am not convinced that anything fundamental has changed.

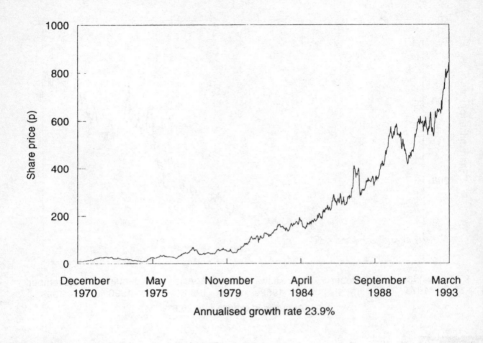

Figure VI.3 **Kwik Save, December 1970–March 1993**
Source: Datastream

John Menzies

✳ **EXAMPLE** Another impressive retailer, though of a different ilk, is **John Menzies**, which together with WH Smith is the largest distributor and retailer of newspapers and magazines in the UK. Many parts of its business enjoy high local market shares, it is highly cash positive, and has grown its share price at nearly 30% per annum since 1978 (see Figure VI.4).

All of the business examples discussed above have been focused fairly tightly on one or two market sectors. But there are examples of good businesses too among industrial conglomerates, where the key considerations are business selection, performance improvement, financial control, and cost reduction. All of the good conglomerates have a finely honed business system which they impose on all of their acquisitions and which results in superior performance. Two which have the best and longest

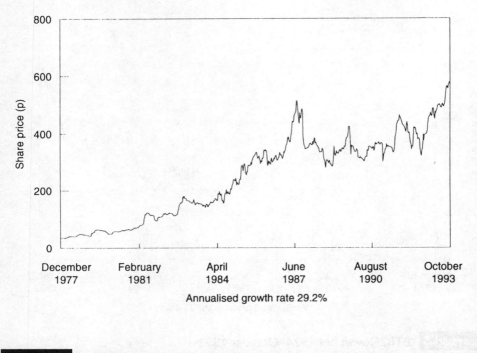

Annualised growth rate 29.2%

Figure VI.4 John Menzies, December 1977–October 1993
Source: Datastream

stock market records are **BTR** and **Tomkins**. As shown in Figure VI.5 BTR can boast a record of 36% share price growth since 1975, while Tomkins weighs in with a 40% annual appreciation since 1981 (see Figure VI.6).

There is, of course, no guarantee that the future will be as glowing as the past, and some analysts have major reservations about Tomkins since its takeover of RHM. The past record, however, has certainly been impressive.

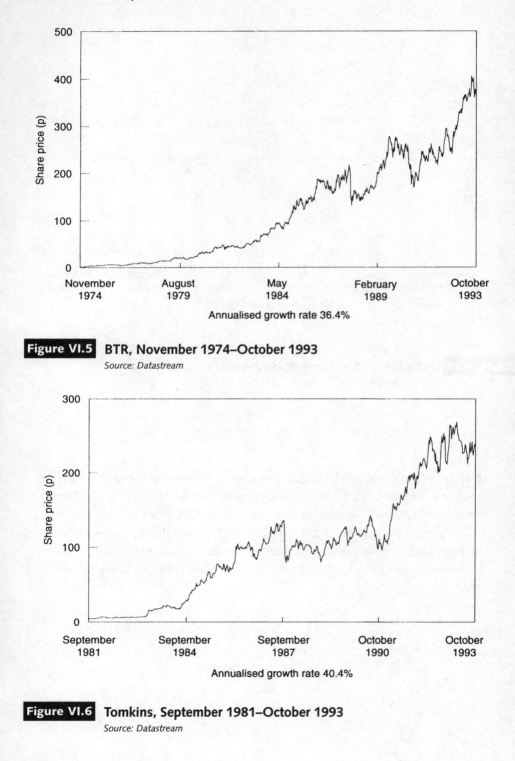

Figure VI.5 **BTR, November 1974–October 1993**
Source: Datastream

Figure VI.6 **Tomkins, September 1981–October 1993**
Source: Datastream

My final example of a good business is the merchant bank **Schroders**.

Schroders

Merchant banks are by nature opportunistic and prone to periods
of good and bad luck or good and bad market conditions. Never-

EXAMPLE ✱

theless, each merchant bank has its own culture and ability to attract talented
individuals, and this often endures for surprisingly long periods of time.
Schroders has a very attractive ethos and its leaders are highly commercial. This
has been reflected in superior stock market performance over the part quarter
century, as shown in Figure VI.7. The fact that a merchant bank has been able to
show an annual rate of growth of 29% for 25 years certainly demonstrates the
power of a good business, even in highly turbulent markets.

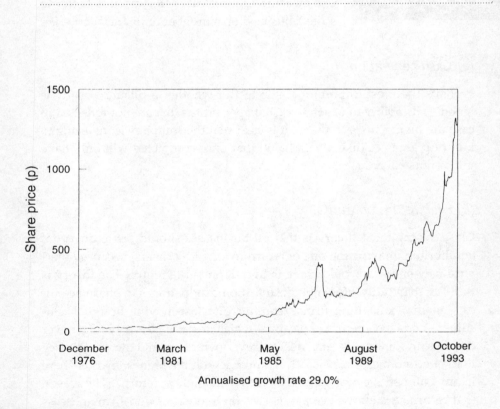

Annualised growth rate 29.0%

Figure VI.7 **Schroders, January 1977–October 1993**

Source: Datastream

HOW TO IDENTIFY AND TEST FOR GOOD BUSINESSES

Good businesses have a number of characteristics which can be used to identify possible candidates and then test whether they really are 'good':

1. Financial attributes

As the name suggests, good businesses should have attractive financial attributes. Different writers will stress different financial parameters here, and to some extent it depends upon the accounting systems used, which vary from country to country and also over time. Slavish adherence to one measure can mislead here, and it is better to score a business on a number of financial criteria:

> It is better to score a business on a number of financial criteria.

(a) Cash generation

Perhaps the most important single test of whether a business really is 'good' is its ability to generate cash. Paper profits that are not reflected in cash are highly suspect, unless it is clear that the company is investing to build up an asset (like a data bank) that once completed will only have minor renewal costs.

(b) High return on capital

Classical capitalist theory is that all businesses should settle down 'at equilibrium' making the rate of return required by savers, because otherwise new entrants would come in and depress the return. The theory is fine but, thankfully, life is not like that. Some industries like pharmaceuticals, media, consulting firms, retailing, and fast-moving branded consumer goods have returns on capital which are well above average: over decades (in some cases centuries) and everywhere around the world's free market economies. Likewise, the company with the highest market share in any competitive system tends to have the highest returns. The reason that returns are above average is that the industries and firms possess some degree of monopolistic or oligopolistic power that is difficult or impossible for either regulators or competitors to erode. Whatever the reason, if a firm has high return on capital and has had for a long time, there is a prima facie case for saying that it is a good business, and is always likely to be a good investment.

(c) Stability of profits and cashflow over time

Some good businesses do suffer occasional dips as a result of the economic cycle or mismanagement, but very few good businesses have very volatile earnings. Look for a long (i.e. 5–10 year) record of stable or increasing profits.

2. Business franchise and high relative market share

A good business must have the sort of franchise referred to in point 1 (b) above, that is, it must have some degree of monopoly power. This can derive from an obvious physical monopoly, such as being the only newspaper in town, or a monopoly in the psyche, such as being the only supplier of Filofaxes or Heinz baked beans.

When thinking about business franchise, there are two key questions to ask:

- Does the business have something that other businesses do not have, like a brand or physical proximity or some emotional appeal, that means that it would naturally be the first choice of its customers, even if its prices were a little bit high?
- Can this advantage be defended against a competitor who sets up alongside the company: in other words, is the source of advantage structural rather than simply temporary?

Good businesses will always have a high share of their markets relative to their competitors: in other words they will be the leaders or close to the leaders in the businesses generating most of their profits. (Note that absolute market share measured in percentages is not a helpful measure here, as a 20% market share could be bad news if there is a competitor with a 40% share, but would be very good news if the nearest competitor had only 5%.)

The high market share may not show up in the statistics because the company may have a niche which is not well documented. For example, Lea & Perrins has a very high relative market share in the UK and most former Commonwealth markets in Worcester sauce, which is a distinct segment separate from other sauces like tomato ketchup, which is dominated by Heinz (both Heinz and Lea & Perrins are very profitable as a result). Or a company may have the highest share of business in its local area, or a very high share of a particular type of customer.

Not all definitions of a market to demonstrate high share are valid. To make economic sense, the definition of the market must enable a company to have either higher prices, or lower costs, or both, as a result of its specialisation (this is why high market share is correlated with high profitability). For example, a specialisation in high performance sports cars is a valid segmentation for Ferrari, because it is able to charge higher prices relative to competition. Likewise, Ford before the Second World War was able to attain economies of scale by providing cars 'any colour you like provided it's black', and attain lower costs as a result. Today the economics of manufacturing cars make it foolish only to offer cars of one colour, because the loss in sales and scale from this move in a market used to choice of colour would not be balanced by the (only slightly) lower costs from just painting in one colour, and so this would no longer be a valid basis for high relative market share.

> ...... Another useful test is whether the high market share can be defended against competitors. ....

Another useful test is whether the high market share can be defended against competitors. If a product can be easily imitated, has no brand protection, and does not have economies of scale or barriers to entry (like the need to make an investment in machinery or expensive marketing) then a high market share is worthless. For example, a hairdresser that does not have a distinctive brand and where the cost of setting up a shop is low, would find it difficult to defend a high market share in a profitable local area, because there would be little to stop another hairdresser coming in and providing an equivalent service. It is a good exercise to think about whether the business really has definable barriers to entry, like a respected brand, control of the channels of distribution, a low cost position, technology, a reputation for customer care and service, geographical barriers, or simply physical assets that would be too expensive for a competitor to replicate. If there is high relative market share in its important markets, and if you can define barriers to entry, it probably is a 'good business'.

3. A winning culture

One of the most important reasons why companies can beat their competitors and keep on having better profit growth than the average lies in the company's culture. Fortunately for the astute investor, this trait is not looked for by the majority of investors, but is fairly easy to recognise.

As an example, compare Marks & Spencer with British Home Stores. Why is Marks & Spencer able to have very much higher profitability? There is nothing in their strategy which, in theory at least, could not be imitated by British Home Stores. They are both large mass market retailers with similar premises in similar locations. They both have access to the same suppliers and the same technology. But the reason that Marks & Spencer does better is that it has a distinctive, winning culture, which fires up its employees and results in excellent buying, demonstrable care for customers, value for money, a lean operating structure and attention to detail.

Many other examples could be given, like Rowntree and Mars. Both are companies with large market shares and powerful brands: Rowntree's Kitkat being comparable in terms of sales to the Mars and Twix bars. But Mars has the more distinctive and relentless winning culture, and has demonstrated higher profitability and growth over a generation.

Because it cannot be easily measured, and because a winning culture is actually fairly rare in the UK (the same is not so true in America, and not true at all in Japan), this way of finding good homes for investment is not much used. In my opinion, however, it is the most reliable test for identifying 'good' companies. Whereas it is possible to have a good company which does not have a winning culture, it is very rare to find a company with a winning culture that is not a 'good' company in which to invest.

If it is so important, how do you recognise a company which has a winning culture? (We have touched on this already in Way V above (page 172), so skip the rest of this section if you have already read that chapter). It is not too difficult, though it may require a visit to the company (if its employees are not in frequent contact with the public). The test is simply how a company's employees behave. Are they enthusiastic about the company? Do they bubble over with enthusiasm for their jobs? Do they move quickly and with a sense of inner purpose? Do they work well together in teams? Are they willing to 'try harder' even if it means some personal sacrifice? In other words, do they enjoy their jobs and care about how they do them? If the answer is yes, their firm has a winning culture.

> **It only takes a bit of common sense to identify whether or not a firm has a winning culture.**

If the answer to these questions is no, or not often, it does not.

You can often judge by telephoning a company and seeing how the phone is answered, or by walking into a firm's reception and seeing how you are greeted and how fast people walk around! It only takes a bit of common sense to identify whether or not a firm has a winning culture.

You should also see whether the firm's main competitor or competitors have a winning culture. If two such companies confront each other, like Coca-Cola and PepsiCo, the beneficial effect of a winning culture can become somewhat muted. What you really want is to find a company with a winning culture confronting another where the people lack enthusiasm for the jobs. If you know just this much about the company then you are well on the way to identifying a good long-term investment.*

4. Alert management

Good companies will usually have good, alert management. This is often more difficult for an outsider to judge, and actually less reliable as an indicator of a 'good' company than the test of a winning culture discussed immediately above, but it is still worth using as a test, particularly if you have a company that passes the other tests but does not appear to have a winning culture. A company with good financial attributes, high market share, a definable franchise and barriers to entry, may still be a 'good' company even if it has a stuffy or bureaucratic culture, providing the management know what they are doing.

If you know something about an industry, try to structure an excuse to talk to a potential investee company's top management. Test whether they are fully aware of the trends in the industry. See whether they are proud of their company's strong point, but not defensive or blind to its defects. Check that they are aware of the threat from serious competitors and know a lot about what competitors are doing. Probe whether they really know what their customers want (and if you can cross-check this some of the same customers, do so). See whether they are lean and hungry, or complacent and sitting on their laurels. Are they introverted and immersed in

---

* For a much fuller account of the importance of culture in corporate performance, see *Wake Up and Shake Up Your Company* by Richard Koch & Andrew Campbell (Pitman/FT 1993).

their company's and industry's ways of doing things, or open to what they could learn from other firms and industries? Are they arrogant or objective?

And, perhaps most important of all, do they set an example of hard work in the service of the firm and shareholders, or are they on a gravy train and prepared to reap the inheritance dealt them? Are they restless and ambitious for the firm, or just self-interested? Personal ambition is no reliable guide here. A clever and moderately unethical manager may manipulate his firm's accounting, postpone investments, sell market share, cut discretionary marketing investment, raise prices and do a thousand and one things to improve short-term results at the expense of the

What you should be looking for is dedication to building something for the company and leaving behind a legacy of achievement for the firm.

long-term position of his firm. Such a manager may even achieve the difficult task of turning a good company into a bad one. What you should be looking for is dedication to building something for the company and leaving behind a legacy of achievement for the firm.

Sometimes a young company has all the attributes of a good company – good financial results, a leading competitive position, and a winning culture – but is still managed by a founder who lacks professional management skills. The time to invest in such a company is just after the founder has left or ceded management control to a good, alert professional manager. This is an almost foolproof buy signal, as in the case of Filofax discussed above.

A SHORT GUIDE TO BAD BUSINESSES

There are many businesses which are neither 'good' in the sense used above, nor 'bad' in the sense used below, but simply mediocre. You should therefore not use the test below as (by exception) and indicator of a good business. But just for fun, and to help you screen out some businesses in the early stages of trying to find good businesses, here goes with a list of the attributes of bad business:

1. High debt

Any good business should be cash positive and normally have only moderate gearing. Any business that has a lot of debt is likely to be bad,

> ..... Avoid anything that is a legitimate target of 'green' campaigns: the greens will win in the end. ....

because it may not be able to generate enough cash to build a reasonable balance sheet. For the same reason, a debt burden that is rising (except as a result of an acquisition) is usually a signal of deteriorating inherent performance.

2. Cyclicality of earnings

All businesses are affected to some degree by the economic cycle, but businesses like construction, property and capital goods manufacturers which are very cyclical are best avoided.

3. High labour cost content

Any business based in the West that has a high proportion of its value added in labour is bound to suffer progressively greater competition from low labour cost countries in the Far East, Eastern Europe and elsewhere. Low end textiles is a good example: avoid any company which cannot charge a premium price.

4. Extractive and primary processing industries

Heavy chemicals, steel, mining and such like are also best avoided. In any cases there is overcapacity in the industry and new investment cannot earn a reasonable rate of return.

5. Companies vulnerable to tighter environmental standards

One clear (and desirable) trend today is towards ever tighter environmental standards. This is another reason to avoid some of the companies listed above, such as those handling toxic chemicals. This can also affect other industries, however, including insurance and heavy industry generally. Avoid anything that is a legitimate target of 'green' campaigns: the greens will win in the end.

The only exception is companies like the privatised, monopoly utilities (water, electricity, and, whatever the regulators say, gas) that are able to pass on enhanced environmental costs in higher prices. Many of these are in fact undervalued 'good' businesses.

6. Industries targeted by the Japanese as 'strategic'

There is no magic about Japanese industrial success: it is the result of long-term investment horizons, attention to what customers want, and a relentless will to win. There is nothing inevitable about Japanese success in any sphere if met by an equal or greater degree of such commitment. Yet such commitment is rarely forthcoming, and as an investor you don't have to bet on it. The odds are against Western success in any such case and the price at which companies exposed to Japanese competition sell does not adequately reflect this handicap. Any industry where the Japanese are aiming at global market leadership is therefore to be avoided.

Take the example of Porsche. In the early 1980s Porsche was dismissive of the danger from Japanese car makers, who were firmly anchored in the lower (and middle) market segments and had no reputation or brand name in sports and performance cars. An unwary investor might have believed that Porsche was a good business, with high market share, a high price premium, and an installed base of loyal customers. But an astute investor, even then, would have found out that companies like Mazda had targeted this industry as the next stage of their world domination of the automotive industry. No-one today would dismiss Japanese competition

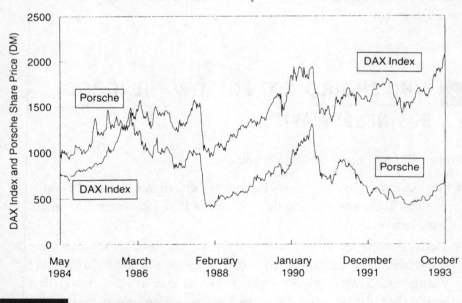

Figure VI.8 **Porsche, May 1984–April 1992**
Source: Datastream

to Porsche or other Western sport car providers (see Figure VI.8). In the future, industries targeted by companies from other Asian countries (including China) may become similarly vulnerable.

7.   Companies with incompetent management

It never ceases to amaze me how many companies, including some quite large ones, actually have incompetent management. We discussed how to probe management's competence above. Always avoid such companies until competent management is installed: and possibly even then, because the damage incompetent management does to a company is often long lasting and difficult to root out. Like buying a used car, always be suspect of a company which has had a bad steward, even if he has long since departed.

8.   Companies with short-termist, grasping or unethical management

Again, we have discussed the symptoms of these diseases above. Do not touch them with a bargepole. Even if the managers involved are competent and intelligent (or perhaps especially in this case), they will do permanent harm to their companies. Over the long haul, these will always under-perform.

WHO SHOULD NOT FOLLOW THE 'GOOD BUSINESS' WAY?

You should *not* choose this Way if you are:

- *Illiquid.* Even good businesses can under-perform for extended periods of time. Therefore you should only invest if you can afford to take a long-term view.
- *Fickle.* For the same reason: you must be prepared to stick to your selections. This may leave you with a boring portfolio that doesn't change much. Most people will not care, as long as it is appreciating nicely. But if you want to make regular and frequent investment decisions this may not be the Way for you.

- *Nervous.* Similarly, you must not get upset if your investment does go down in value. With some other Ways in this book you are encouraged to cut your losses on loss makers. This Way is genuinely for the long term and involves a commitment to your selections, unless there is evidence that you were or are wrong about them being 'good businesses'.

- *Highly risk averse.* If you do choose really good businesses, the risk should not be too high. But the risk may be higher than other approaches as a result of having a smaller number of stocks in your portfolio. It is not easy to find really good businesses, and having identified one you should plan to hold a reasonably large stake for quite a long time. Overall this is a medium-risk approach.

Advantages... *of backing 'good businesses'*

1. This Way is based on very sound principles and yet offers an approach neglected by the generality of investors. The tests given above should lead to a high-quality portfolio which can be safely and profitably held for the long term.
2. If the investigation is conducted competently, there should be little ambiguity about whether or not a business qualifies as being 'good'.
3. If a big enough portfolio of such businesses can be identified, this should be a relatively low-risk Way.
4. After the initial investigation, little time is required supervising the portfolio.

Disadvantages... *of backing 'good businesses'*

1. Good businesses are few and far between. You may have difficulty in identifying enough of them.
2. You may end up with fewer investments than is desirable for spreading risk.
3. The initial investigation can be hard work.
4. Once you have your portfolio, you may get bored by the lack of churning activity.

WHO IS THIS WAY BEST FOR?

In contrast to some others, this Way may suit almost any personality type. It may appeal particularly to Type 2 people, however, because the selection process is inherently analytical. Although this process is not excessively quantitative, it does require the ability to understand a balance sheet and assess the financial characteristics of a business. On the other hand, picking your shares also requires some contact with people in the company and some evaluation of the management. This rules out the armchair investor, the bone idle and the incurably shy.

> This Way rules out the armchair investor, the bone idle and the incurably shy.

This is a method best suited to the patient and intelligent all-round investor. If you are such it should serve you very well.

➤ Overall evaluation

This Way is the one that most closely resembles Warren Buffett's highly successful approach. The criteria proposed for investment include all of the important tests used by Buffett, plus my own passionate belief in the importance of a firm's culture in determining long-term returns. The criteria are mainly derived from industrial reality rather than financial manipulation; they have a long and rich heritage in terms of theory and observation. Even those who opt for a different Way may find it helpful to apply these criteria before finally deciding on their investments.

The main attraction of this Way is that it can lead to a very high-quality portfolio which still should yield returns far above the average. The prerequisites are a degree of skill and a lot of objectivity and common sense in applying the criteria.

WAY VII

Value investing

This Way is for patient and analytical investors (Type 2) who have a reasonably good knowledge of accounting.

The philosophy of value investing

Does value investing work?

What's the catch?

Anatomy of a value investor

The rules of value investing

Value investing and the stock market cycle

Who is this Way best for?

Overall evaluation

THE PHILOSOPHY OF VALUE INVESTING

Value investing is one of the oldest, most rational and most respected share selection techniques. It rests upon that most simple and venerable law of capitalism: buy low and sell high. Value investing is certainly a philosophy, and sometimes a religion. At its simplest, value investing rests on four fundamental precepts:

1. The value of shares rests on the value of the total company. The latter can be calculated by reference to its financial characteristics.
2. The market price of shares and companies is a result of supply and demand and can reflect irrational concerns driven by fashion, animal spirits, hope and fear.
3. Therefore, it frequently happens that the market price of a company or the stock market as a whole is either above or below the true, calculated value which results from examination of the underlying financial characteristics.

Value investing is certainly a philosophy, and sometimes a religion.

4. Sooner or later, however, the market reverses itself and tends to revert towards the true value, although in doing so it will often overshoot, before reversing itself again.

The value investor believes that he or she knows the true value of companies better than the market. For this reason companies can often be bought at below their true value. But since the true value will become increasingly apparent over time, and since the variations in value follow a cyclical pattern, there will come a time when a share bought at below its true value can be sold at, or above, its true value.

The value investor is aware, of course, that the 'true' (calculated) value of a company can shift over time, as its financial characteristics change. But at any one time a value investor can always know two numbers: the true value of a share, and its actual market price (or market 'value': although the purist value investor tends to use the word 'capitalisation' rather than 'value' to denote the market price, since the purist does not believe that the market price need bear a close resemblance to true value, so that 'market value' involves a misuse of the word value). The rule for the value investor is simple: buy a share if its true value exceeds its market price, and sell if the reverse is true.

DOES VALUE INVESTING WORK?

Amazingly, yes. Most religions rely on faith rather than proof. But value investing has a well-proven historical track record.

The eternal high priest of value investing is Benjamin Graham, who published its Bible, *Intelligent Investor*, in 1949. Graham kept refining his rules for value investing throughout a long career, but it is evident that he prospered as a result of practising what he preached, as indeed have Warren Buffett (who described his approach as '85% Ben Graham') and his followers. A number of American academic studies have been conducted that clearly validate Graham's approach. For example, Professor Oppenheimer constructed a 'Grahamite' portfolio for 1973–81 which would have returned 25% compounded annually, way above the US stock market average.

WHAT'S THE CATCH?

If value investing works, and is a mechanical process, why doesn't everybody practise it, so that the stock market prices come into line with the true, underlying value calculated by the value investors?

There are three important objections to value investing that help to provide the answer:

1. The theory of value investing is not convincing to most investors. Given that investors determine the price of shares through supply and demand, there will be long periods when value investing values for shares will bear little resemblance to reality (they are generally lower than the real market prices). For all but the true believers and those with the longest time horizon, therefore, value investing provides no real clue as to where prices will move, and other approaches are therefore more popular.

2. The idea that the value of a company can be determined by a few financial rules strikes most managers and investors as far too theoretical, dogmatic, and faintly repugnant. It smacks of predestination, denying free will. Companies are living, breathing entities whose fate and future lies in the hands of managers and depends on how well they do and on the firm's ability to learn and develop. The idea that a bunch of desiccated accountants and analysts can know the value of the firm better than people who understand the industry and its players can be difficult to swallow.

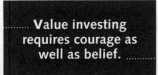

.... **Value investing requires courage as well as belief.** ....

3. The value investing rules rest on past behaviour. But what if the future is different from the past – will the old rules still work? If the behaviour of financial markets shifted for some reason, the rules of value investing would need to be revised and those who had made investments based on the old rules would be left high and dry, having bought shares on a yardstick that was no longer valid.

More practically, there are four reasons why not everybody is a value investor:

1. It's hard work, requires a knowledge of accounting and quantitative skill, and the sort of personality that likes and believes in the value investor's 'fundamentalist' approach.
2. For long periods of time, the approach is practically useless, because it would tell you to buy few or no shares, rating most of the whole market as overvalued.
3. As a consequence of the point above, value investing can only be profitably followed by very long-term investors. It can be dangerous to the wealth of those who may need to go liquid quickly, because periods when the value investor receives 'buy' signals are often those of major recession and stock market depression and volatility, and prices often continue to sink long after the 'buy' signal starts flashing.
4. Value investing requires courage as well as belief. It may fly in the face of observed behaviour for long periods of time. The value investor needs the serene certainty that sooner or later the market will come to its senses. (It has to be said, it always has done so, so far!)

ANATOMY OF A VALUE INVESTOR

This investment approach requires, above all others discussed in this book, a particular cast of personality. Look down this profile of the value investor, and decide if it is for you:

- *The value investor is an analyst.* If you did not emerge as predominantly a Type 2 personality, you are unlikely to become a good value investor.

- *And a rationalist.* The value investor has great faith in numbers and in reason. He or she believes that the financial world, like the physical one, revolves around certain immutable laws.

- *The value investor has a trace of arrogance and dogmatism.* He or she believes that generally, if the sums have been done correctly, history will vindicate him or her, whatever the current trends. To take a political analogy, the value investor has a contempt for opinion polls (like Lady Thatcher) rather than being a devotee (Harold Wilson, John Major).

> Patience and steadiness are value investor traits.

- *The value investor is cautious, calculating and prone to say the glass is half empty rather than half full.* He or she looks for downsides, fatal flaws and defects, is sceptical and difficult to convince. The value investor never jumps on bandwagons. Patience and steadiness are value investor traits. He or she will rarely, if ever, be accused of excessive enthusiasm or optimism, except for the cause of value investing itself.

- There are exceptions, but *the value investor is much more likely to be an introvert than an extrovert.*

- *The value investor is always intelligent.* (But a majority of intelligent people are not value investors.)

Do you recognise yourself here? If not, even if you believe in the approach, you will not enjoy being a value investor and I would not recommend that you follow this Way. If you attempt to, you will probably backslide at some point, to your financial cost. (I will own up, and say that I am not a value investor, for this very reason, even though I do believe in it. My own personality is far from that outlined above.)

If I have not succeeded in putting you off value investing, you may want to know how to go about it!

THE RULES OF VALUE INVESTING

Like most religions, value investing has a number of variants and competing sets of rules. For the sake of simplicity I will restrict myself to two:

Graham's Main Rules

This is a summary of the rules he used for most of his career. They have the advantage of being well validated (in the US market) and the disadvantage that they are rather stringent, and a British investor today would find few companies passing these tests (and then rather odd ones that most people might want to avoid). It is worth reading these, however, even if you don't intend to use them, because they give you a feel for the value investing religion and its underlying principles.

Graham's Value and Safety Criteria

More useful in practice than the rules Graham used during most of his life are those he used towards the end of it, which were published posthumously in 1977. It is these rules that Professor Oppenheimer used retrospectively to show a 25% compound annual return between 1973 and 1981. It has to be said, however, that the rules are still pretty tough.

Graham's Main Rules

1. The Adjusted Net Assets Rule

Buy if the total market capitalisation of a company is only two-thirds (or less) of the company's net quick assets (i.e. net assets, but not counting stock on the grounds that it may be hard to sell and not worth anything), but then deducting from the assets (giving no value to) plant and equipment, property, goodwill or indeed any assets that are not cash or debtors. (This is a very stringent rule indeed in practice. It would be practically useless in the UK stock market in 1994)

Sell when the company's market capitalisation has reached the level of 100% of its adjusted net assets as defined above. This would produce at least a 50% gain (and no wonder, since the price was so cheap to start with!). Graham tested this rule on all possible US investments of this type between 1945 and 1976 and found it produced almost 20% compound annual return.

2. The Earnings Yield Rule

The earnings yield is the reciprocal of the price earnings ratio (if a company is on a 20 times PE, that is, its market capitalisation is 20 times its earnings, its earnings yield is 5%; on a 10 PE, the earnings yield would be 10%; if the PE is 5 times, the earnings yield would be 20%). Graham's rule is that, provided the company's total debt does not exceed its tangible net worth, it is appropriate to invest if the earnings yield is at least twice the yield on top quality bonds.

At the time of writing the yield on top quality bonds is approximately 7.5%, so the earnings yield required would be 15%, and to qualify on Graham's test, a share would need to trade on a PE of 6.7 or less (100 divided by 15 is 6.7) to qualify.

The *Investors Chronicle* has suggested using the redemption yield on medium-dated government stocks as a proxy for the yield on top quality bonds. This results in a slightly less stringent test, as the yield on gilts is currently (December 1993) 6.5%, leading to a 13% earnings yield requirement (or a PE of 7.7x or lower). It is easier to find the yield on government stocks than UK corporate bonds and you may want to use the former as your benchmark, but if you do, remember that it will give a slightly higher allowable PE ratio than Graham intended, so you should round it down slightly or at least apply it very strictly.

Many shares that pass this test (i.e. are on low PEs) would not pass the proviso above that the company's net debt should not exceed its tangible net worth, so it is important to remember that a company must pass both tests.

3. The Dividend Yield Rule

This rule also requires that the companies debt be less than its net worth, but in addition focuses on dividend rather than earnings yield. (The dividend yield, usually called simply 'yield', is the current value of dividends divided by the current price of the shares.)

The rule is that the share's dividend yield must be at least two-thirds of the high quality bond yield. With this yielding 8%, a dividend yield of at least 5.35% is required. Many shares currently trade on yields above this level, some of which are basket cases but many of which also satisfy the rule that debt is less than net worth.

Rules for selling under all three cases

Graham proposed for shares bought under rules 1, 2 or 3 above that they be sold if one of the following events occurred:

(a) if the shares rose 50%, or
(b) if the dividend was passed (and therefore the yield fell to 0%), or
(c) if the market price became more than 50% above the hypothetical purchase price, as justified by the relevant rule, or
(d) in any case, if one of the above events had not happened already, after two years.

Graham's Value and Safety Criteria

As far as I know, Graham was never an examination paper setter, but perhaps he should have been. His 1977 test required a minimum of *one value criterion* (out of a possible five) *AND one safety criterion* (also out of a possible five).

Value Criteria

1. The earnings yield should be at least twice the high quality bond yield.
2. The share's PE ratio should be less than 40% of the highest PE it had recorded in the previous five years.
3. The share's dividend yield should be at least two-thirds of the high quality bond yield.
4. The firm's market capitalisation should be two-thirds or less of its tangible book value.
5. The firm's market capitalisation should be no more than two-thirds of its net current assets.

Safety Criteria

1. Total debt must not exceed book value.
2. Current assets should be at least double current liabilities (the current ratio must be at least 2).

3. Total debt should be less than twice net current assets.
4. Earnings growth over the past ten years must have been at least 7% per annum compounded (roughly, earnings today must be at least double what they were ten years ago). Note that in periods of high inflation this rule becomes meaningless and provides only illusory safety; a rule requiring a *real* return of at least, say, 3% per annum would have to be substituted (e.g. if inflation averaged 12%, the average return required would be 15% per annum).
5. Earnings must be relatively stable, as defined by the requirement that in the last ten years there may only have been two (or fewer) occasions when earnings fell by 5% (or more).

The following examples of shares that passed Graham's Value and Safety Criteria show that his method is also appropriate for the British stock market. In each case, good returns can be obtained in the medium and long term. The 'buy' signal from the Grahamite tests occurred at the start of the period shown in Figure VII.1

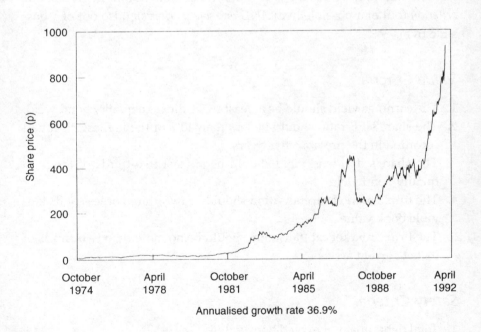

Annualised growth rate 36.9%

Figure VII.1 Glaxo, October 1974–April 1992

Source: Datastream

The dying words of a character from one of Anita Brookner's novels are 'Never sell Glaxo'. This was certainly a good motto for the 18 years up to the start of 1993, as Figure VII.1 shows. By the end of 1992 a value investor would certainly have sold Glaxo, and its performance since has been relatively poor.

Another share the value investor would have bought at the end of 1974 and held at least until 1987 (and bought again after the Crash, selling again in 1990) is Hanson (Figure VII.2). Interestingly, the Hanson return over this period was even better than the Glaxo one, turning in a stunning average annual increase of 39%. It is hard to imagine any novelist advising you to 'never sell Hanson' but this would have been a good policy for more than a dozen years.

Guinness is another share where Graham's tests would have been satisfied both in 1975 and in 1981. The returns from either of those dates to July 1992 (when the tests would definitely have told you to sell) have been impressive, notwithstanding the Saunders affair (Figure VII.3).

A value investor would have had occasion to buy TI Group from mid-1984 to mid-1986. The increase in value since, under the inspired leadership of Sir Christopher Lewinton, has been good (Figure VII.4).

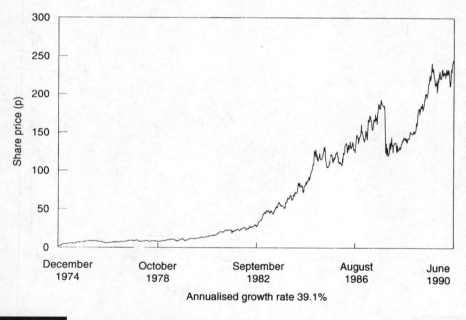

Annualised growth rate 39.1%

Figure VII.2 Hanson, December 1974–June 1990
Source: Datastream

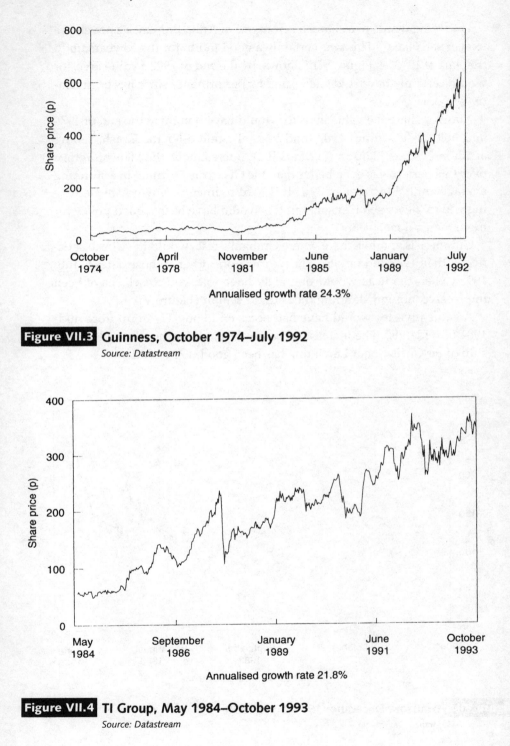

Figure VII.3 Guinness, October 1974–July 1992

Source: Datastream

Figure VII.4 TI Group, May 1984–October 1993

Source: Datastream

Another engineering company, Wagon Industrial Holdings, would have been a value investor's 'Buy' during 1984, and a clear 'Sell' during July and August 1987. The share price appreciation during this period was a stunning 66% per annum (Figure VII.5).

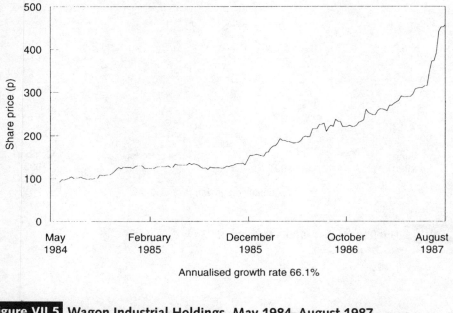

Annualised growth rate 66.1%

Figure VII.5 **Wagon Industrial Holdings, May 1984–August 1987**
Source: Datastream

In the past three years it has become increasingly difficult to find shares that qualify under the value investing rules. One share that did, in mid-1990, was HP Bulmer, the cider company. Since then the shares have gone up by 32% per annum (Figure VII.6).

It is intriguing, and may well be highly significant, that during the research for this book the writer could find no single example of a large company that currently satisfied the value investing rules for buying.

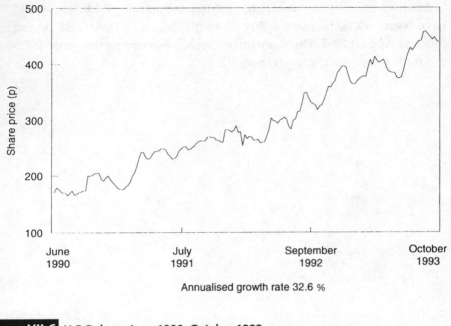

Annualised growth rate 32.6 %

Figure VII.6 H P Bulmer, June 1990–October 1993
Source: Datastream

VALUE INVESTING AND THE STOCK MARKET CYCLE

One characteristic of value investing is that it tends to give more 'buy' signals in bear markets and 'sell' signals in bull markets. For the long-term investor this can be very favourable, as there is great virtue in counter-cyclical investment: for the market as a whole, it has always been true that, at some stage, what goes up must come down, and vice versa.

Yet value investing may lead to periods when (as now) there may be few shares which pass the tests, and those that do may have something very suspicious about them; as well as to periods in bear markets when too many shares pass the tests, thus making it very difficult to follow the purist requirement that *all* qualifying shares be bought (you could end up with very small quantities of lots of shares, with high dealing costs as a result).

There is also a danger that value investing may lead to 'premature' buy and sell signals when the upward or downward trend has gone far enough to trigger the signals but in fact still has a way to go. The long-term investor who is confident of the tenets of value investing may not care, but it can lead to some uncomfortable moments when shares bought as

> ····There is also a danger that value investing may lead to 'premature' buy and sell signals ············

'undervalued' become even more so, and shares sold as 'fully valued' continue their ascent.

✔ Advantages... *of value investing*

1. It is a proven technique based on sound criteria.
2. If the inflexible rules are followed relentlessly, it can eliminate the elements of subjectivity, hope and special pleading that tend to bedevil the private investor.
3. It can lead to well above average returns based on a large portfolio, when the risk should be no more than moderate.

All of these are big advantages.

✘ Disadvantages... *of value investing*

1. It is only for the long-term investor, and preferably the well-heeled investor too.
2. It requires technical skill, as well as patience, faith and consistency.
3. It can lead to periods of prolonged inactivity.
4. It is a desk-based activity and therefore devoid of the human interest that some other investment techniques involve.
5. There is no practical or theoretical guarantee against the rules of value investing becoming obsolete (though they have lasted well to date).
6. Value investing may generate too many or too few recommendations for a balanced portfolio. Once you attempt to apply judgment (for example, to limit the size of the portfolio), the objective advantages of the technique become lost.

WHO IS THIS WAY BEST FOR?

Analysts only! See the above section, 'Anatomy of a value investor' (page 204).

► Overall evaluation

A renewed bear market would certainly see value investing enjoying a revival. Value investing is currently a tremendously under-valued technique! As with the stock market itself, the cycle will turn sooner or later.

If you have the right personality and skills, value investing may be the lowest risk Way to achieve markedly superior results.

WAY VIII

Emerging markets

This Way is most suited to well-heeled, long-term investors who are willing to take a risk with part of their portfolio. Type 1 personalities may be particularly attracted.

THE BASIC IDEA

One of the most intriguing investment propositions is to invest in fledgling stock markets in fast-growth economies. The basic idea could not be more simple. Maturity equals low returns. Youth equals high returns. Rarely can an investment idea have more going for it: track record, ideology, economics, the tide of history, an explosion of interest, but early days yet; a combination of reasons to invest that should make the most curmudgeonly investor sing, and the least cautious pause for reflection! It is an idea that the novice can grasp and invest simply, yet also offers scope for the sophisticated investor to develop new and complex routes for outperformance. It is a bandwagon that has only just started in earnest, that everyone can jump on, and perhaps that everyone should! Whether or not you agree with the approach, it is perhaps the most interesting to contemplate of all the ten Ways in this book, because it folds in lessons in history, economics, investment behaviour and politics.

Emerging markets are fast-growth stock markets where the habits of market capitalism are still young and developing. 95% of the value of the world's shares are outside them, in boring places like the US, Japan, Germany, the UK and anywhere that has a stable and well-developed stock market. Emerging markets include most of Asia (except Japan), Latin America, the Indian sub-continent, Africa, Eastern Europe, and fast-growth parts of southern Europe like Greece, Portugal and Turkey. Emerging markets account for only 5% of stock markets globally, but 12% of world GNP and 83% of world population.

WHY INVEST IN EMERGING MARKETS?

There are seven quite compelling arguments in favour of investment in emerging markets. The reasons are higher investment returns, higher GNP growth, low labour costs and gains in world trade share, privatisation, the (apparent) demise of Communism, low price earnings ratios, and

> **The astute investor will be wary of an impending hangover.**

the accelerating flow of cash into these markets. Taken together, these reasons constitute a heady cocktail, though the astute investor will be wary of an impending hangover.

1. Higher investment returns

The recent track record of emerging markets, taken as a whole, is undeniably impressive. In a comparison in the *Financial Times* (8 July 1993), of 54 countries examined, emerging markets took eight out of the top ten positions. Nor is this a short-run phenomenon. Of 17 emerging markets examined from the end of 1984 to June 1993, the average annual return (in US dollars) was 26.4%, compared to 16% in the US, 18% in Japan, and 19% in each of the UK and Germany (see Figure VIII.1). This difference may not sound much, but it means that $100,000 invested in the US (for ten years) would have turned into $441,000, but the same $100,000 invested in emerging markets would have ended up as over $1m, or 236% of the US return. Note that regionally, Latin America did best in Figure VIII.1, with an average annual return of 35%. Chile produced an annual average of 52%, meaning that $100,000 invested ten years ago would have multiplied to $6.58m!

2. GNP growth

The basic reason behind investment performance is the growth of GNP (Gross National Product) or GDP (Gross Domestic Product). There is no getting away from the dominance of this influence. Yes, the share of the national cake taken by capital, labour and government can shift over time, as it did in Britain in the 1970s towards labour and in the 1980s towards capital, but these shifts are essentially temporary and are relatively muted compared to the effect of GNP growth. There is thus an irrefutable and inevitable long-run correlation between investment performance and GNP growth adjusted for population growth. Once this point is accepted, the case for investment in higher growth economies by long-term investors becomes enormously powerful.

Figure VIII.2 shows the average annual real increase in GDP per capita between 1965 and 1992. The same trends for 1992 (actual) and 1993 (forecast) can be seen in Figure VIII.3.

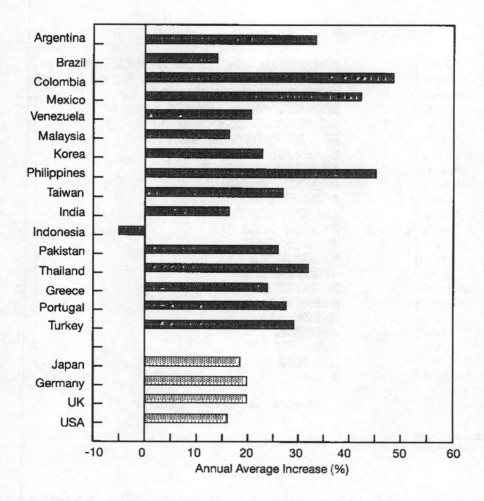

Figure VIII.1 Stock market total returns on a yearly basis from end 1984–June 1993 in US dollars

Source: MSCI and IFC Global Total Return Index including gross income

3. Growth in world market share

Although the correlation between investment performance and growth in GDP per capita is clear, the most important underlying reason for growth in stock market values is growth in the share of world trade or world market share earned by developing countries. This in turn is driven by low labour costs, aggressive management, an outward-looking mentality and cultural/government encouragement of exports.

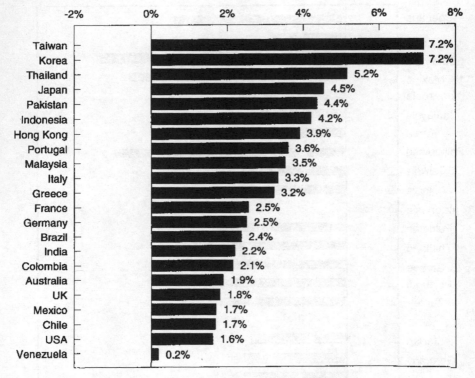

Average annual increase in GDP/capita

Figure VIII.2 Percentage annual change in GDP/capita, 1965–92
Source: Datastream, OC & C analysis

One of the best leading indicators of investment performance is performance in growing world market share. A generation ago, Japan would have been the best example of this. Today, the prize goes to Far Eastern countries like Thailand and South Korea, and those Latin American countries (like Chile) that take pride in the development of an outward-looking capitalist economy.

Before deciding which countries to invest in, check the trend in their share of world trade.

4. Privatisation

Thanks to Peter Drucker's idea and Margaret Thatcher's implementation of it, privatisation, have become a global trend. They will have the greatest influence in increasing the range and size of investment opportunities in the emerging countries. Stock market companies account for an average of 66% of GDP in the UK, USA and Japan, but for only 29% in emerging markets.

> .... **One of the best leading indicators of investment performance is performance in growing world market share.** ....

Countries that take large companies from the state into the publicly quoted sector tend to do so on generous terms for investors. Further, newly privatised companies have a good record of increasing returns, partly because they were so badly managed (from a profit perspective) previously.

The whole stock market should benefit from an increase in the size and liquidity of companies available for investment. In part, this trend should help to prevent a potential quality problem that could arise if a wall of money from developed economies seeks to pour into stock markets with few high-quality stocks.

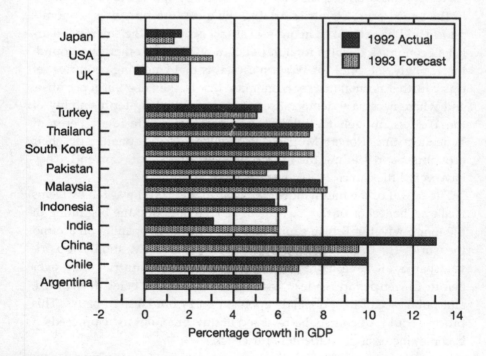

Figure VIII.3 Percentage growth in GDP for 1992 (actual) and 1993 (forecast)
Source: Datastream, OC & C analysis

5. The strange, sudden death of Communism

George Dangerfield once wrote a book about the strange and sudden death of Liberal England in the early twentieth century. At the end of the century, Communism appears to be committing suicide in a not dissimilar way. Arguably, the consequences of the latter for investors could be momentous.

> In the emerging markets, economics dictates foreign policy now, not the other way round.

Emerging countries have always needed to attract capital for development. Previously, this could be obtained by a variety of expedients and from a variety of sources. A favourite game was to auction political allegiance for foreign cash from either the Western or Soviet blocs. Once capital was attracted, even from the West, there was no guarantee that it would be wisely spent, that market economics would be pursued or maintained, or that the interests of foreign investors would be respected once the initial cash had been obtained.

Now, perhaps, all this has changed. It certainly appears to have done so in the short term. Countries around the globe are pursuing economic reform and have to do so in order to attract capital. In the emerging markets, economics dictates foreign policy now, not the other way round. Increasingly, the price for Western capital is that emerging countries set up or further normal market economies: that is, they liberalise, privatise, and where necessary democratise to underpin the long-term stability of the Western model. Erstwhile socialists such as President Perez of Venezuela and Robert Mugabe of Zimbabwe, are opening up their economies and leading the charge for Western capital. Currently they have very little choice.

The power of the International Monetary Fund (IMF) was felt by Denis Healey, Chancellor of the Exchequer, in 1986, marking the beginning of the long revival of British capitalism. The same is happening all around the world. The IMF, the World Bank, the US Government, and the top private banks all have more influence on emerging countries than ever before. Currencies are made to float, capital controls are being dismantled, and public sector debt depends upon support from Western banks. This process could, of course, be reversed at any time, but as it proceeds it becomes increasingly difficult to turn back.

The argument is, therefore, that governments in emerging markets are forced to make the 'right' decisions for their economies and, of course, for

Western investors. This could create a virtuous circle, particularly for those who invest now. As capitalist institutions become more entrenched, and democratic government more long standing, the perception of risk in relation to emerging countries will change. International money will flow in, and price earnings ratios will move towards those in developed stock markets.

> ....It is likely that in both the short and the long term demand for shares in emerging countries will grow faster than the supply. ....

Emerging markets will become mature ones, with higher values.

You can evaluate how far you believe this scenario. It may be too good to be true. While you are thinking about it, let me make explicit the final two reasons put forward for investment in emerging markets.

6. The Western wall of cash

There is no doubt that Western (I use this term, inexactly but conveniently, to include Japan) institutions are underweight in emerging countries, or that this is beginning to change. Mark Donegan of Morgan Grenfell estimates that less than one-seventeenth of one per cent of Western institutional funds are invested in emerging markets excluding South East Asia, but that by the year 2000 this proportion may have risen to 30%. Whether or not you believe in this 500-fold increase, it is clear that investment interest is rising exponentially at the moment. New emerging market funds are being launched every month in London and New York, and investment advisers are beginning to take this area much more seriously. Some of the closed funds are selling above their net asset value, signalling excess demand.

Despite the privatisation trend, it is likely that in both the short and the long term demand for shares in emerging countries will grow faster than the supply. Their result is very likely to be a significant increase in prices, although doubtless with some wild swings along the way. The trend is likely to continue and accelerate until and unless political instability re-emerges, the progress towards market capitalism is reversed, economic growth levels off or share prices begin to approach Western levels of valuation.

7. Emerging country shares are good value

Differences in accounting standards make exact comparisons very difficult, and there is very considerable variation across sectors and countries, but it is clear that emerging country shares as a whole are priced considerably lower than in developed countries, whether the measure is historic price earnings ratios or market-to-book ratios. In many countries leading company shares can be bought on historic multiples of 5–10 times earnings, under half the current levels in the US or the UK.

Perhaps this is appropriate: there is clearly much more risk. But there is also hugely greater growth potential. The prospective price earnings ratios two or three years out sometimes fall below five. If you believe the 'golden scenario' painted above, earnings and price earnings ratios will rise, potentially causing a multiplication of value over a few years. This is clearly what has happened in Chile, for example: you simply cannot grow earnings at 50% per annum for ten years across an economy as a whole, but with price earnings ratios rising as well, it is possible for a whole stock market to grow at this rate for a decade. If you pick the right future markets – and the 'golden scenario' implies that there will be many more Chiles in the future – the rewards could be tremendous. Of course, if you are wrong, or the golden scenario turns out to have feet of clay, you could lose most of your investment.

IS HISTORY ON YOUR SIDE?

This is a book on investment, not history or politics, but you simply cannot decide whether to invest in emerging markets without polishing your own personal crystal ball.

The 'golden scenario' is certainly seductive, and can point to some tempting examples. Once upon a time the US was a hair-raising investment prospect: politically unstable, war-torn, economically volatile, devoid of decent accounting standards, full of unscrupulous robber barons, racked by racial tension, fast growth certainly, but not to be trusted. Those nineteenth- and twentieth-century investors who risked it nonetheless, on the whole have done very well. The value of the US stock market in recent years has only been rivalled by Japan, which is the other prize example. Only a generation ago, Japan was an emerging market. If you had noted the progress of small companies like Honda, Mitsubishi, Sony or Toyota you could have bought their shares of price earnings ratios of around five, and multiplied your investment by now several hundreds or even thousands of times.

Some emerging countries clearly do emerge, to the great satisfaction of most investors. But if you look ahead a generation (say, to 2025), will Russia be a stable, prosperous market economy? India? Brazil? Venezuela? Indonesia? China? Zimbabwe? The question can be reduced to individual countries, and this is useful, because you must see whether you can visualise the transition and think it reasonably likely. But it is also a question of the tide of history. A long historical perspective is necessary too. We have referred above to an estimate that 30% of the world's stock market value by the turn of the century will be in markets of negligible value today. This may seem a wild prediction, but in Edwardian Britain 25% of UK institutional money was tied up in Latin America – and nearly all of it lost! Similarly, nineteeth-century investors were once hot on China and pre-1917 on Russia too.

> Think whether you believe in Capitalist Progress or Hobbesian Regression, and invest, or not, accordingly.

You have to ask yourself: were the investors before the Russian Revolution just unlucky, or foolish? Is Communism dead, or just in a cyclical downturn? Will China become a capitalist country and a source of profits for Western investors, or upset the whole 'golden scenario'? Will Latin America ever really place a high value on repaying foreign capital? And so on. Do not invest in emerging markets just because it is becoming fashionable. Think whether you believe in Capitalist Progress or Hobbesian Regression, and invest, or not, accordingly.

CAVEATS

There are six principal reasons against investment in emerging countries:

1. Quality

It is difficult to be sure that the companies you are investing in will be high quality in terms of their market positions, predictability of earnings, or management. There are few stockbroking analysts or fund managers in the world who really understand the position of even the large companies in large emerging markets. When it comes to a small company in Ecuador you really are taking pot luck. You may end up investing in many companies of very poor quality.

2. Spreads and liquidity

Emerging markets are very imperfect, which is a major disadvantage as well as potential advantage. Spreads on all stocks are well above those in developed markets, and may widen dramatically as well as downward if you try to sell. A quote of 22 (to sell) and 28 (to buy) is not untypical, which means that an investor has to see an appreciation of 27% just to break even! This is good for brokers, but not for investors.

3. Three-fold risk

You face three different and compounding sorts of risk: company risk, country risk, and currency risk. Any one of these going wrong could sink you.

4. Market volatility

Emerging markets yo-yo in a dizzying way. For example, between January 1992 and mid-1993, the Brazilian market oscillated between plus 200% and minus 90% of its original value! These movements make the UK, US or Japanese 'crashes' of October 1987 look like mild corrections.

5. Remember the South Sea Bubble

Much of the current weight of money going into emerging markets is based on 'flavour of the month' considerations and fashion rather than fundamental analysis. This may drive prices higher for a time, but if the fundamental support is missing there may be horrendous setbacks, and the entire premises behind investment may turn out to be false.

6. Will you be able to take profits?

It is easy to find willing overseas takers for your equity money, but will you be able to get the money out in due course? Confiscation is always a popular remedy when unstable governments are in a fix, and from the investor's viewpoint it matters not at all whether the motive (or excuse) is nationalism or socialism: either way, you lose.

HOW DO YOU INVEST IN EMERGING MARKETS?

By now, you may no longer be interested and want to move to another chapter. But if you are still contemplating investment in emerging markets you will probably be asking how this can be done. It is actually not as difficult as you might think, but you need to be aware of the different routes in, which may mean all the difference between high positive or high negative returns. There are four generic ways:

- investment direct, by selecting markets and shares yourself;
- by giving a large discretionary lump sum to a stockbroking specialist;
- by buying relevant investment trusts; and
- by investing in unit trusts.

These are in descending order of difficulty and risk, and for nearly all private investors the practical choice today is between the last two ways.

1. Investment direct

In theory, you could decide to invest directly in leading shares of the countries you select. Leading emerging country brokers such as Barings, James Capel or Morgan Grenfell issue research documents on such shares and would be willing to buy them for you, provided you deal in sufficient volume. This approach is not recommended, however, unless you are (1) rich; (2) risk seeking; and (3) knowledgeable about the particular countries and companies in which you plan to invest. This should rule out nearly everyone!

2. Discretionary stockbroker account

Specialist stockbrokers in emerging countries deal almost exclusively for institutional clients. Most of them will, however, make an exception for the occasional 'retail' client (i.e. you or me) provided you have at least £500,000 to invest in emerging countries and are willing to give them discretion as to the investments. If you can find a good broker and develop the right relationship, this can be a cheaper and more personal method than the two below – but, again, very few people have the spare half million or so to invest in this speculative sector (bear in mind that with only 20% invested in emerging countries, half a million pounds here means a total share portfolio of £2.5m, which is rather more than most of us have).

3. Investment trusts

If you look in the daily *FT* Investment Trust price section (in the main body of the London Share Service), you will find around 40 trusts which can be loosely described as dealing in emerging countries. Some cover all emerging markets (e.g. Govett Emerging Markets, Kleinwort Emerging Markets, Templeton Emerging Markets), some are regional (e.g. Latin American Dollar Fund), and some are country specific (e.g. Abtrust New Thai, China Investment Trust, Drayton Korea, Siam Select, Turkey Trust, Brazilian Investment Trust).

There is nothing to stop you putting together your own portfolio of investments in these investment trusts simply by buying the shares, in the same way that you would buy BT or Shell. If you plan to do this, the best thing to do is to select 20 or so of the trusts that sound of potential interest to you and order the annual reports and other marketing literature from the trusts, as well as asking for data from the Association of Investment Trusts and reading relevant articles in the financial press. You can then decide which countries and trusts to invest in.

This approach is only recommended for the relatively sophisticated investor, but it has a number of advantages as against method (4) below. There are three main advantages of investing in relevant investments trusts:

- You can exercise much more personal control over your investments. Although you are investing at one remove, you can select and change the mix of countries and fund managers at will, depending on performance and your own view of country prospects.

- You can select funds which are currently selling at a discount to their net assets. The *FT* tells you the approximate discount (or premium) to net assets each day. Whereas one fund may be selling at a small discount or even a premium, there are funds which sell at a 10%, 15%, 20% or even greater discount from time to time. If you are prepared to invest in that particular country or region, this is clearly better value than buying shares directly or via a unit trust which will price itself in relation to net assets.

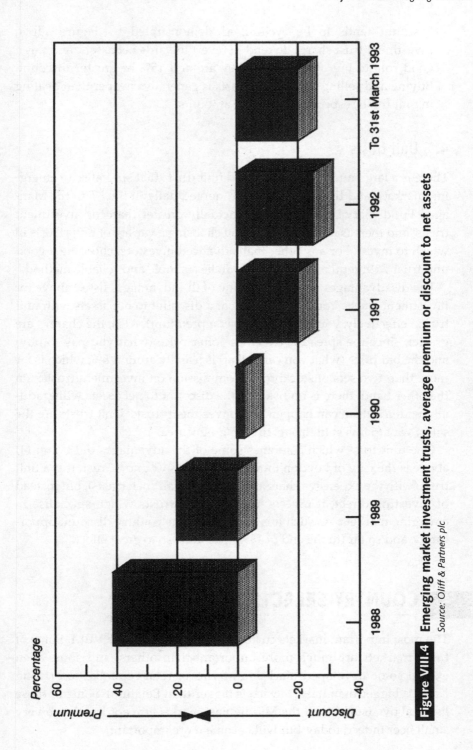

Figure VIII.4 Emerging market investment trusts, average premium or discount to net assets

Source: Oliff & Partners plc

- Discount tends to be cyclical, as demonstrated by Figure VIII.4. Investment trust shares do tend to revert towards net assets, and it is a good rule to buy funds when they are at a 15% or greater discount. Buying and selling investment trusts is generally cheaper than dealing in unit trusts, especially for larger amounts.

4. Unit trusts

There is a large number of authorised unit trusts that specialise in emerging markets, and their prices are also quoted daily in the *FT* in the Managed Funds Service. The choice is actually greater than for investment trusts, and there is nothing to stop you choosing a variety of units trusts in which to invest. For any other than advanced investors, choosing a good unit trust with reputable managers can be a simple and reliable method.

The disadvantages are the other side of the advantages listed above for investment trusts. You cannot invest at a discount to net assets with unit trusts (effectively, you will always pay a premium). Also, the charges are greater, since the spread between the offer price (what you pay to buy) and the bid price (what you can sell at) is usually around 6%, which is far more than two sets of stockbroker commission on investment trusts. On the other hand, there is no risk that the discount to net assets will gradually widen, which can happen with investment trusts. Unit trusts are the safest way to invest in this relatively 'go-go' area.

One unit trust which combines some of the advantages of (3) and (4) above is the City of London Emerging Markets Country Trust. It is a unit trust (with the expensive charging structure of all such trusts), but instead of investing direct, it invests in investment trusts which specialise in emerging markets. As such it is able to play the country discount opportunity, and so far (to the end of 1993) has done so to great effect.

COUNTRY SELECTION

The most important markets currently are shown in Table VIII.1. Some of these markets are much more important than others, and some even exceed some developed markets in terms of total capitalisation (Hong Kong is bigger than Italy; Mexico is bigger than Belgium). Some of those listed above (such as all the Middle East markets except Israel) are very small beer indeed today, but will become more important.

Table VIII.1

Latin America	Argentina, Brazil, Chile, Mexico, Venezuela
Asia	Hong Kong, Indonesia, Korea, Malaysia, Philippines, Taiwan, Thailand
Indian sub-continent	India, Pakistan, Sri Lanka
Middle East	Egypt, Israel, Syria, Jordan
Africa	Zimbabwe, South Africa
Southern Europe	Greece, Portugal, Turkey
Eastern Europe	Hungary, Poland

Beyond these markets, others may develop into quite important arenas: in Latin America, Peru is growing fast, followed by Ecuador and Bolivia. In Africa, markets to watch include Botswana, Ghana, Kenya, Morocco and Zambia. China and Russia of course remain potential giants. The definition of emerging markets will change over time, with new entrants and some maturing markets dropping out of most definitions.

How do you decide which countries to invest in? You could choose to cover all fronts and select trusts appropriately: this is the easiest route, and perhaps the safest. But you may want to exercise some discretion. One way would be to look at the track record of the countries or regions involved. Towards the beginning of the chapter we provided some data on the record of 17 leading emerging country markets from 1985–93 in US dollars. The best countries (in descending order) were Chile, Mexico, Philippines, Colombia, Argentina and Thailand. Figure VIII.5 summarises this data into regions. You can then decide whether the future will be different from the past. My own guess would be that Asia and Eastern Europe will offer both higher returns and a safer ride than Latin America, the Indian Sub-continent or Africa, but I could easily be wrong. A personal list of interesting countries for the next five years would include Peru, Ecuador, Bolivia, Colombia, Greece, Portugal, Turkey, Korea, Philippines, Thailand, Zimbabwe, India, Morocco and Egypt, but with the portfolio weighted towards the Asian countries (perhaps half of total assets) to decrease risk. Those who want a higher risk/return profile could omit the Asian countries.

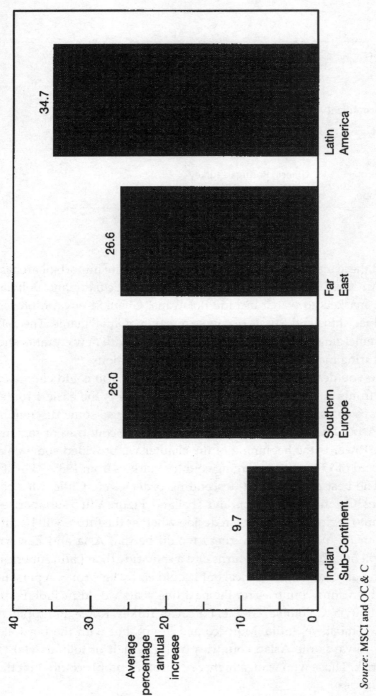

Figure VIII.5 Average annual increase in share prices by region

Source: MSCI and OC & C

✔ Advantages...   *of emerging countries*

1. This Way offers you the chance to cash in on investment in countries which have higher GNP growth and growth in the private sector than the UK, the US, or most of Continental Europe. Ultimately, investment returns are determined by GNP growth.
2. The track record of most emerging markets (and certainly a portfolio of them) over the past two decades is far superior to that of investment in the mature markets.
3. Investment via unit trusts (and for more advanced investors, investment trusts) is relatively simple and straightforward. This is not the case with some of the later Ways in this book.
4. In the short- to medium-term, accelerating investment demand for emerging countries is very likely to drive prices up, possibly quite fast and quite far.
5. Arguably, the decline of Soviet Bloc Communism has marked a watershed in the economic and political development of most emerging countries, and the road to market economies has become clearer, quicker and more certain. This step function reduction in risk for investors in emerging countries may not yet have been built into share valuations.

✘ Disadvantages...   *of emerging countries*

1. The historic return may have been higher, but so too was the risk. Sooner or later risky investments go sour. This time may come during your investment period.
2. It takes an act of faith to believe that all or most of the emerging markets in which your fund managers may invest will in fact develop into stable, capitalist, market economies.
3. These investments are inherently expensive to make and manage, with wide spreads and heavy management costs in terms of travel and communications. These costs appear relatively unimportant when the markets are going up, but can become prohibitive when markets are sliding.
4. The short-term risks are huge, as market volatility is great and liquidity is poor to start with and can dry up in a bear market.

5. Over the very long haul, investment in exotic foreign locations has had a very mixed record. No one has yet demonstrated that over a century or two returns in these riskier markets have been higher than at home. The great danger is that you may not be able to get your money out, as a result of war, economic collapse, revolution, a change in regime, or capital repatriation restrictions. There are many examples of investors and lenders acting like lemmings in providing funds to such markets when such is the fashion, but living to regret it bitterly afterwards.

WHO IS THIS WAY BEST FOR?

To enjoy this investment, it helps if you have an interest in one or more of the potential countries or regions, and contacts who can provide data on economic and political developments there are useful. This Way is definitely best suited to those with larger amounts to invest, since it is high-risk and should only constitute a small part of your total portfolio (to begin with). Because of the short-term risks, it is definitely better for the long-term investor.

Those of a nervous disposition should invest elsewhere.

In terms of personality type, this Way can suit any of our Type 1, 2 or 3 categories. The chances are, however, that it will appeal more to Type Ones (visionaries) than to the others. Those of a nervous disposition should invest elsewhere.

Unusually for an investment which has an established and superior track record, this Way does not require any special skills, since specialist fund managers are available and are in the best position to assess which countries and companies to pick. On the other hand, those who want to practise their skills in quantitative analysis or country risk assessment have plenty of grist to their mill.

▶ **Overall evaluation**

The decision is yours, and it is very likely that you have come down very firmly on one side or the other. This is definitely a high-risk Way, and should only be used for a fraction (up to a fifth) of your starting portfolio.

It is always dangerous to go with a swelling trend, but my judgment is that the intellectual balance lies firmly with the protagonists of emerging markets. I believe that in the long haul economics will dominate politics, except where rampant nationalism holds sway. For the brave, this Way has much to commend it.

→ **an update**

As hinted, 1994 was a bad year for most emerging markets and 1995 mixed at best. There are signs that emerging markets are returning to favour but it will continue to be a bumpy road.

WAY IX

Opening the SLITs: capital shares of Split Level Investment Trusts

This Way is for sophisticated investors who like complex calculations (Type 2 personalities).

WHAT IS A SPLIT LEVEL INVESTMENT TRUST (SLIT)?

An investment trust is a quoted entity which invests in other companies on behalf of investors who do not want to manage their own money. The managers of the investment trust buy and sell shares (sometimes in other quoted companies, sometimes in unquoted companies, sometimes in both) and very often specialise in a particular region or type of share (such as small companies or technology companies). Shares in the investment trust are then bought by private investors (and sometimes by other investment institutions) in the normal way, and the price of these shares reflects not only the underlying value of the shares in the investment trust, but also the normal laws of supply and demand for the investment trust.

Investment trusts can be valuable where, as in the case of the emerging markets discussed in the last chapter, the type of shares in which the investment trust invests are both difficult for private investors to buy and sell as easily themselves, and also are shares that perform well as a class. Investment trusts that specialise in particular types of foreign shares or in unquoted companies also have a role. But for most readers of this book, investment trusts will generally be of limited interest, since you are likely to do better by investing your own money. This is not just my own opinion: most investment trusts sell at a discount to the value of the assets, reflecting the fact that investors place a *negative* value on the manager's services: the discount is saying that the managers subtract more value than they add.

> Investment trusts will generally be of limited interest, since you are likely to do better by investing your own money.

There is, however, a special type of investment trust that will be of interest to analytical private investors. This is called a Split Level Investment Trust (what I call a SLIT), which divides up its shares into different classes, with different claims on the overall assets of the trust. As explained below, the class of shares which is of most interest in these SLITS are the capital shares (sometimes also called the ordinary shares), which have the most uncertain return of all classes of shares, but can potentially offer spectacular returns.

A MIRACLE OF FINANCIAL ENGINEERING

The invention of the Split Level Investment Trust was one of the most simple but most significant innovations in investment engineering. This relied upon the insight that investors' requirements were different: some wanted income, some a low risk and predictable capital gain, others the possibility of dramatic capital gain. Previously, these different requirements had to be satisfied from different underlying shares or other instruments. The Split Level Investment Trust turned all this on its head, by providing different classes of shares in the same investment vehicle.

The idea was cunning, simple, analytically flawless, and probably well ahead of its time, since most SLITs rapidly proceeded to sell at a discount to net assets in the time-honoured fashion of investment trusts generally. Now that SLITs are commonplace, there are signs that the real virtues of SLITs are coming to be appreciated by the investment community, ever a suspicious and conservative beast.

> The SLIT is one of the most useful tools available to sophisticated, analytical investors aiming for superior investment performance.

The SLIT is one of the most useful tools available to sophisticated, analytical investors aiming for superior investment performance. We will explain shortly exactly how SLITs work, but for the moment let us focus on our particular quarry within the SLITs: the capital (or sometimes called the ordinary) shares of these trusts.

In its pure form the capital shares of SLITs pay no income and are the riskiest class of shares in the trust. They come last in the queue for paying out a trust's assets when it is wound up: after all the other classes of shares. But – and here is the mouthwatering upside – they get everything left over after the predictable claims of the other classes of shares have been satisfied. The capital shares are the ultimate capitalists in an investment trust, and all other forms of 'capital' are in effect loans of one sort or another which, if funds are available, will get their fair and specified due, but no share of super-profits. If there are any, all super-profits go to the holders of the capital shares.

You might think that such shares would be in great demand, given the upside. But, praise be to the god of investors, this is not the case. Most institutions are leery of SLIT capital shares, a few because they still do not understand or trust them, many because of the volatility and risk inherent in them. As a result, most capital SLIT shares sell at a thumping and quite undeserved discount to their true current value. Many theoreticians and investment advisers would disagree with this last statement of mine. I will represent the case against these capital shares, I hope, fairly and dispassionately. But in my view, the discount is a quite irrationally extreme reaction to risk, and offers the prudent and quantitative investor a market anomaly which may not exist in future years, and one that can hold the key to beating the market handsomely.

> **Most institutions are leery of SLIT capital shares.**

There are two legitimate uses of SLIT capital shares: one short to medium term, and one long term. The first, and most risky use, is as a bet on upward movement in the stock market as a whole (or in whichever mix of stock markets the investment trust invests). SLIT capital shares are a leveraged bet on the direction of the market and will respond well and in an exaggerated form to an upward (or downward) movement in the market. Although risky, the investment is much less risky and much better value than investing in traditional or traded options or in the 'index' bets provided by bookmakers. More risky, but not necessarily less lucrative. The average SLIT capital share rose 65% between 1 January 1993 and 20 August 1993, when the FT-SE 100 (Footsie) index hit a new high. Many capital SLIT shares did much better.

> **Most capital SLIT shares sell at a thumping and quite undeserved discount to their true current value.**

The second and longer-term use of these capital shares depends on confidence that their managers can increase value over the life of the trust. The long-term investor should still not ignore the short-term prospects, taking care to buy when the market is depressed or at a plateau, or else investing steadily over a long period to iron out short-term fluctuations. This long-term investment also carries a reasonably high degree of risk, but made wisely can involve a highly favourable relationship between risk and reward. I will explain how, where and why later. For the moment, let us look at examples of the performance of such shares (see Figures IX.1–IX.6).

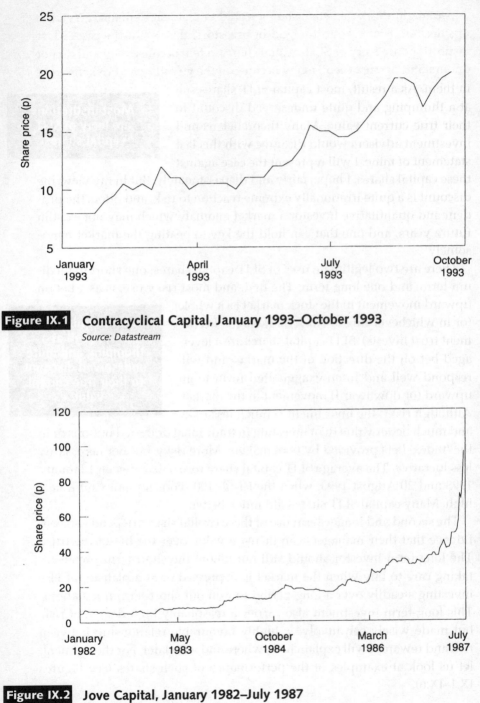

Figure IX.1 Contracyclical Capital, January 1993–October 1993

Source: Datastream

Figure IX.2 Jove Capital, January 1982–July 1987

Source: Datastream

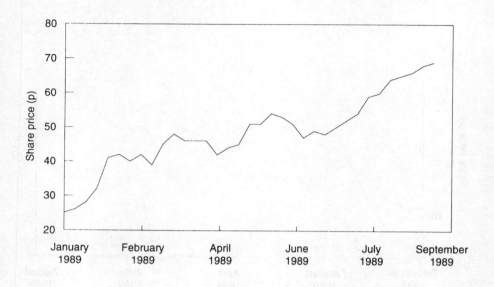

Figure IX.3 **Scottish National Capital, January 1989–September 1989**
Source: Datastream

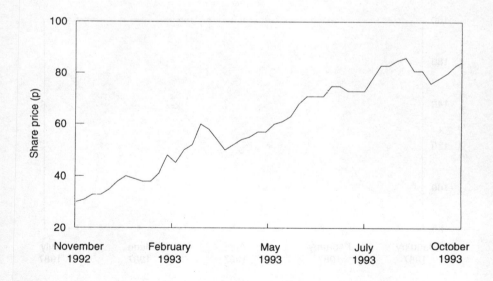

Figure IX.4 **Jos Holdings Capital, November 1992–October 1993**
Source: Datastream

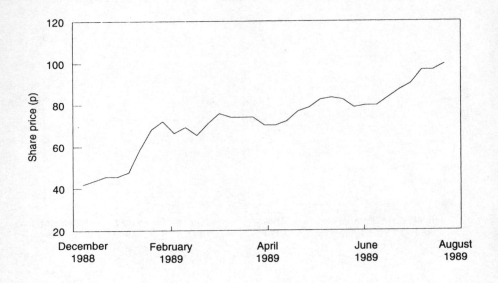

Figure IX.5 River and Mercantile Trust Capital, December 1988–August 1989

Source: Datastream

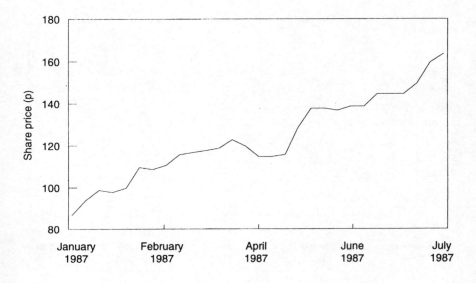

Figure IX.6 Yeoman Capital, January 1987–July 1987

Source: Datastream

Table IX.1 summarises the average annual percentage increase in the value of these shares over the time periods shown in Figures IX.1–IX.6.

Table IX.1

	Annualised growth rate %
Jove Capital	73.2
Jos Holdings Capital	217.5
Contracyclical Capital	220.7
Yeoman Capital	225.7
River and Mercantile Trust Capital	312.6
Scottish National Capital	374.4

HOW SLITS WORK

The investment managers of a Split Level Investment Trust operate in the same way as a normal unitary trust to select appropriate shares in the chosen field of specialisation and increase the net assets of the trust as much as possible. They are trying to bake as big a cake as possible. The difference from a unitary trust comes in how the cake is 'split' at the end of the trust's life, when it is wound up and the investors in the trust paid out.

Within a SLIT, there are two, three or four different classes of shareholders who are treated quite differently when the pay-out comes, and who hold different bits of paper with different values until this great day comes. The different classes of shareholder have different orders of pay-out and different rules governing what they get.

The Zero Coupon Preference Shareholders (holders of what are called simply the 'Zeroes') receive no income over the life of the trust but have the first call on its assets at dissolution. If there are enough assets, they receive a predetermined amount laid down in the articles of the trust (so many pence per share on dissolution). If there are not enough assets to meet this amount, the Zero holders still receive whatever is available, with nobody else receiving anything. But once the Zero holders have received their due amount, that is it: they get no share of super-profits. The Zeroes are attractive to higher income people who do not want income but do want a fairly predictable yield to maturity, which can be taken as a capital gain at the end of the period (or, by selling the shares, at any time in between).

Next after the Zero holders in the queue for assets on dissolution are either holders of *debentures* or *stepped preference shares*. Terms for these holders vary according to the particular trusts' articles, but the key point is that they receive the next layer of available assets, after the Zero holders, up to an amount again predetermined. They will also receive a measure of income (increasing over time in the case of the stepped preference holders: hence the 'step') along the way.

Next come the holders of *income shares*. (Sometimes there are only income and capital shareholders in trusts which do not have Zeroes, debentures or stepped preference shares.) The income shareholders, as the name suggests, have a right to dividends during the life of the trust, and again a predetermined amount or share of profits on winding up.

Once all these claims have been satisfied, however, all of the assets on dissolution of the trust go to the *capital share* holders. This amount can be a lot, a little, or nothing at all. If the trust has performed poorly or in a mediocre way, there will be little or nothing left for the capital shareholders. But if the trust has done very well, they will make a killing.

Some SLITs also provide *package units*, which are simply a pro-rata mixture of the different classes of shares. This offers investors the ability to rebundle the SLIT into an unsplit (conventional) trust. The most useful aspect of this for our purposes is that it provides an easy way to look up in the *FT* the discount or premium attaching to the trust as a whole.

Note that some SLITs have a slightly different structure, with the role of capital shares being fulfilled by 'ordinary' shares. These have exactly the same attributes as capital shares, coming last in the queue but taking all the super-profits, except that ordinary shares may receive some dividends during the life of the trust. These dividends are not normally very large, however, and are certainly not the principal reason for people to invest in them. I therefore include such ordinary shares in SLITs in the same category as capital shares. This is imprecise, but more useful than precision. One example of 'pseudo-capital' shares is TR Technology Ordinary Shares, whose performance has been illustrated above (sees pages 19–20).

VALUATION OF CAPITAL SHARES

Valuation of a SLIT as a whole is easy: the reference point should be its net assets at any particular time. Of course, since the trust has a life to run, this is not necessarily a guide to its future value. The trust may sell at a discount to net assets if the market believes that the trust's managers will subtract more value than they will add (relative to the market) during this time, or at a premium to net assets if the belief is that they will do better than the market. Historically, most trusts have sold at a small (but recently narrowing) discount to net assets.

> **Historically, most trusts have sold at a small (but recently narrowing) discount to net assets.**

More problematic, interesting and potentially profitable is the valuation of different classes of shares within a SLIT, and especially the valuation of the capital shares. The straightforward, common sense valuation is to look at the current net assets of the trust attributable to each class of shareholder, that is, what they would get if the trust's game of musical chairs stopped now and each group received its entitlement up to now. This can be easily calculated, and indeed is available each day in the *FT*, under the NAV ('Net Asset Value' column), provided as an approximate guide by NatWest Securities.

For the trusts as a whole, the NAV is usually quite close to the market (share) value quoted at the time. For example, on 17 September 1993, the TR Technology Package Units had a middle market price of £26.50, a Net Asset Value of £27.14, and therefore a discount of net assets of 2.3%. At the same date, a more recent and highly regarded trust, the M&G Recovery Fund, saw its package units selling at 136p, their Net Asset Value at 128p, and therefore the market price at a 6.5% premium to NAV.

Now comes the really interesting part. Despite the close relationship between SLITs' market value as a whole and their Net Asset Value, the capital shares usually sell at a significant or even very large discount to **their** NAV. In the two cases quoted above, the market value (share price) of the ordinary TR Technology shares (effectively the capital shares) on 17 September 1993 was 94p, compared to a theoretical NAV of £2.31, implying a whopping 59% discount. On the same date the M&G Recovery Capital Shares were priced at 23.5p against a NAV of 73.2p, an even greater discount of 66.5%, despite the premium to NAV enjoyed by the trust as a whole!

These are not isolated examples. The average discount for capital shares (including ordinary, pseudo-capital shares) relative to the Net Asset Values on 17 September 1993 was 47.4% for the 26 such shares quoted in the *FT*.

WHY DO CAPITAL SHARES SELL AT A LARGE DISCOUNT TO NET ASSET VALUE?

This anomaly in the valuation of capital shares is not new, and has been commented on by many observers. The basic reason for the apparent undervaluation is the fact that the trusts are not about to be wound up, and the current value of the capital shares could be undermined by future events. Whereas the future value of the capital shares is wholly uncertain, some other classes of shares, notably the Zeroes, are bound to increase their claims on the funds' net assets in the future, according to a predetermined schedule. It is clear that the discount to net assets for capital shares is generally much greater for those SLITs that have Zeroes in their capital structures.

The existence of the other classes of shares, especially the Zeroes, means that the funds have to increase their net assets at a particular rate, sometimes quite a high rate, to justify the current share price of the capital shares, or, indeed, to pay the capital shareholders anything at all. A more conservative way (some would say, the correct way) to value a capital share is therefore to allow for the ultimate claims of other classes of shareholders when the trust is wound up, rather than looking at the current value, which relies on the wholly false assumption that the game of musical chairs can be stopped now. On this basis, most capital shares sell at a large *premium* to their (final) NAV. You can view the market price of a capital share, intuitively, as a compromise between this conservative view and the current net asset view.

In a moment we will look at how analysts actually do value SLIT capital shares, and at the opportunities implied. I cannot resist, however, attacking here the whole basis of the conservative valuation of capital shares on their final Net Asset Value. Since the point of capital shares is that they are high risk, their value should be based upon a future expected value (discounted back to the present), which should take into account many scenarios of what the future value should be and weight them according to their probability. This, plus a modest discount for extra risk, can constitute the only theoretically valid way of looking at the capital shares. The current NAV is a valid (although not the only) guide to the value of the capital shares, because it implicitly looks at performance of the fund and different classes of shares to date, and says simply what would happen now if the fund's final date happened to be today. This is not a perfect measure of value, but it is a relevant and defensible one.

By contrast, the conservative measure is completely illogical, because it implicitly assumes that the fund's total value between now and its liquidation remains the same as today, but that the claims of other classes of shareholders continue to augment. The proponents of this measure would reply that this is normal actuarial practice, and the whole point about it is that it is conservative. I do not find this convincing. You could make other 'conservative' assumptions, such as the value of the total fund actually declining, or that there will be nothing left for the capital shareholders at the end of the day, which would place a zero value on the shares. These other conservative assumptions are intrinsically no less logical than the final valuation method, which to my mind holds one dimension of time static (the total value of the fund is frozen at its current value), while allowing a corresponding dimension of time (the claims of the other shareholders) to roll forward in the normal way.

> ....**The current NAV is a valid (although not the only) guide to the value of the capital shares** ....

It is my personal belief that in the future the net asset valuation of capital shares will be seen as the best single benchmark, and if I am right this would mean, over time, a massive revaluation of these shares. In my view the correct valuation of these shares should be a compromise, not between the current NAV and the conservative view, but between these two views and a third view based on the upside scenario that is equally probable as the conservative view (but in the opposite direction). I believe that the practical results from this tripartite valuation would tend to cluster not far away, on average, from the NAV. I recognise, however, that my view is rather extreme, or at least unusual. It is based on my belief that the rate of future increases in stock market values (especially for funds specialising in smaller companies and emerging countries) will be at least as fast as it has been in the past. You may reject both my view and its premise totally, however, and still emerge as an interested investor in capital shares. I will now explain how the analysts who specialise in SLITs value the capital shares, before elaborating a little (mercifully, just a little!) on my own proposed method of valuation.

HOW DO ANALYSTS VALUE CAPITAL SHARES?

The methods used by specialist analysts of investment trust shares (of whatever class) are logical and instructive. Their main thrust is to calculate the yield that each class of shares would enjoy (the 'gross redemption yield', which means the average annual rate of return before tax on the shares from now until the trust is wound up, including both capital gains and any income received *en route*) under different assumptions about how fast the trusts' total assets grow.

✳ EXAMPLE To take an example quoted in the *FT* (25 September 1993) based on data from the Association of Investment Trust Companies, the capital shares of Contracyclical Investment Trust on 31 August 1993 were quoted at 20p. If you believe that the trust would not grow its assets at all between then and maturity (in over seven years' time), then the capital shares would become worthless. If you believe that the trust will increase its net assets by 1.8% per annum, you would obtain 20p on redemption (i.e. a gross redemption yield of 0%), not a very exciting prospect given the fact that you would receive no dividends and that seven years or so of inflation would be eating away at the value of your original 20p. But if you believed that the trust's assets would increase by 10% per annum (which is not too demanding, implying with 4% average inflation a real gain of 6% per annum, for example), the capital shares would yield an annual return of 25% per annum.

Two other examples also quoted in the *FT* article help to make the point about geared returns. A 'risky' capital share, Scottish National, was quoted at 34p on that date. If the fund's assets failed to grow at all over the remaining five years of its life, the capital shares would be worthless. If the assets grew at 4.4% per annum, the shareholder would recover the original 34p (again somewhat ravaged by inflation). But if the fund grew at 10% per annum, the gross redemption yield would be 49%.

A less risky capital share, Aberforth Split Level, had a less pronounced upside and downside. If the assets of the fund did not rise at all over its near 11-year life, capital shareholders would still gain a 4.2% gross redemption yield, about enough to compensate for inflation. If the fund's assets grew at 10% per annum, the gross redemption yield for capital shareholders would be 14.8%: a quite decent return, but well below the 25% for Contracylical Capital shareholders or 49% for Scottish National shareholders.

Analysts speak of the 'hurdle rate' for capital shares, which means the rate of growth of assets for the trust necessary to return the current share price, when the trust is wound up. In these three examples the hurdle rate was 1.8% for Contracyclical, 4.4% for Scottish National, and minus 3.8% for Aberforth Split Level (the latter meaning that the assets of the fund could afford to decline by nearly 4% per annum, and the capital shareholders would still get their money back).

The relationship between the fund's rate of growth of assets and the returns (gross redemption yields) for capital shareholders is shown in Figure IX.7 (as of 31 August 1993).

HOW CAPITAL SHARES SHOULD BE VALUED

The right way to value capital shares (for an investor unafraid of risk) is to look at a frequency distribution of the possible asset values of the fund when it is wound up, to assign probabilities to each outcome, to work out the implied value of the capital shares under each scenario, and then to take the weighted average value. This price should then be discounted by an annual percentage discount to reflect inflation and the added annual return requirement for risk.

> The key judgment, of course, is what the probabilities are for the future asset value of a fund.

The key judgment, of course, is what the probabilities are for the future asset value of a fund. Although the past is not necessarily an indicator of the future, it is probably the best one available. I would therefore propose two measures to help at arriving at a 'base case' for future asset growth of any given trust, viz:

(a) the average annual performance of the trust to date, and
(b) the long-term average rate of growth of assets in the market(s) where the trust invests.

For simplicity, you can then take a 'high' case which represents the 75th percentile of your estimate of possible outcomes, and a 'low' case which represents the 25th percentile. You can then take a simple average of the three estimates to arrive at a 'likely' value for the shares on winding-up.

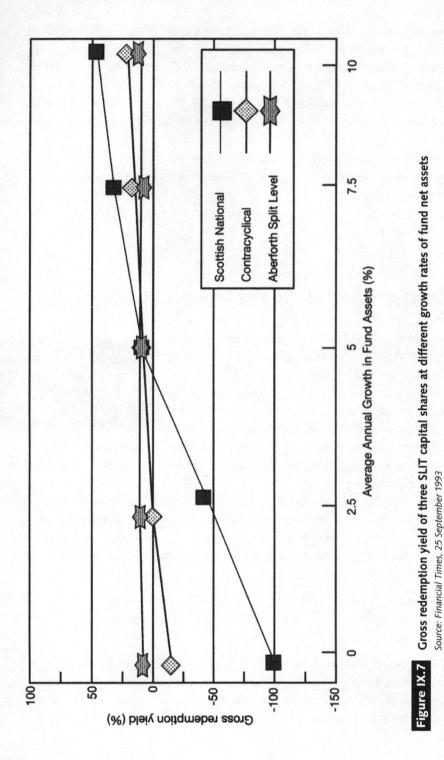

Figure IX.7 Gross redemption yield of three SLIT capital shares at different growth rates of fund net assets

Source: Financial Times, 25 September 1993

You can then calculate the gross redemption yield for each capital share, based on this 'average' outcome.

A final refinement is to calculate the theoretical value today that each share should have, given you own risk-adjusted discount rate. You may find it useful to have three different rates to reflect low, medium and high risk capital shares. For example, for low risk capital shares you may take inflation plus 2% per annum, for medium risk inflation plus 4% per annum, and for high risk inflation plus 7% per annum. If you assumed that inflation would average 4%, then your discount rates become 6%, 8% and 11% respectively.

This methodology will tend to produce higher values than the current share prices, but the extent of the premium to the market value is an interesting additional measure to set alongside the discount to current net assets and the hurdle rate when evaluating which capital shares offer the best value.

TWO WAYS TO USE CAPITAL SHARES

As indicated above, capital shares can be used for short- to medium-term investment, when you expect the relevant market to rise in the near future, or for longer-term investment, when you expect the market to rise on trend for a number of years. Each of these uses requires different checks and procedures.

USING CAPITAL SHARES FOR SHORT- TO MEDIUM-TERM APPRECIATION

Capital shares are a very efficient and low-cost mechanism to bet on short-term market appreciations. Despite this, however, you can easily end up losing nearly everything from this approach. You should only use this method, therefore, for a small part of your portfolio, with money you can afford to lose, and after analysing diligently the prospects for a short-term market appreciation. In plain English: this is, at best, informed speculation (though it can be great fun!).

There are four rules for this approach:

1. Do not buy capital shares while their price is falling

This is not a bad rule for any shares, but it is particularly relevant to capital shares, because they are so geared and volatile. You may think that the shares represent excellent value, but if they are still falling you will be able to buy them cheaper later (and you may be wrong!). It is far better to miss the bottom and buy once the shares have started appreciating again than it is to buy on what you think is a plateau but discover is actually a short rest on the way downhill. A good procedure is to adhere to this two-fold rule:

- do not buy if the current price is below the average price of the last 20 days, and
- do not buy unless the price has been flat or rising for each of the last 5 days.

The more prudent investor should also follow two other rules:

- do not buy until the price has risen for three out of the past five days, and
- do not buy unless the price is at least 10% higher than its recent low.

2. Do not buy capital shares when the stock market is 'overvalued'

This is pretty obvious and banal advice unless we define what we mean as 'overvalued'. We have touched on this subject before (see pages 7–9), but we now need a rather more lengthy digression on the signals that warn of a potentially overvalued market. The short-term capital share buyer, above all, cannot afford to ignore any of these signals. This subject, which is also relevant for the long-term buyer of capital shares, is covered after giving rules (3) and (4) below (see pages 255–261).

3. Buy a portfolio of capital shares

You are running enough risk without betting everything on your selection of the capital shares. Pick at least five shares, and preferably ten, with at least three of them focused on different geographical markets (the UK, one developed market such as the US, and one emerging region or a fund covering all emerging markets).

4. Bias the portfolio towards lower risk capital shares

As a rule, the lower risk ones are those with lower hurdle rates, and the lowest discounts to NAV. Select at least 40% of the portfolio in low risk and 40% in medium risk capital shares. In the example above, Aberforth Split Level would be low risk, Contracyclical medium risk and Scottish National high risk.

> .....The subject of when the stock market is overvalued has attracted an enormous amount of comment and rival statistical explanations. ....

When is the stock market 'over-valued'?

The investor in SLIT capital shares, and especially the short- to medium-term investor, cannot afford to take the chance of buying the shares when the stock market as a whole is at, or near, a peak from which it will fall. You are taking enough risk in buying this class of shares at all; you should not compound this risk by buying when the market might be about to fall.

The subject of when the stock market is overvalued has attracted an enormous amount of comment and rival statistical explanations. None of the theories is guaranteed to be correct; but I have selected three which I believe ought to be respected by any investor, but particularly by the investor in SLIT capital shares (and, to come in the next chapter, the investor in warrants).

The stock market may be about to fall if any of the following three conditions obtains:

Market vulnerability indicator (A): Price earnings ratio

The market may be about to fall if the historic price earnings ratio is 15 or higher
An analysis by Philip Coggan (*FT*, 14 August 1993) of the correlation between the historic price earnings ratio of the FT-All 500 index since 1965 with the gain made by the index over the ensuing year is especially convincing. From 1965 to 1992, the PE varied between 4.0 (1975) and 22.5 (1969). Dividing the PEs into 4 batches, the growth of index for the lowest batch PEs over the following year averaged 32.4%. By contrast, when the PE was at its highest (over 14), the index grew in the next year by an average of only 2.4%.

Interestingly, there were three years when the PE was over 20, and in each case the market fell by over 15% in the next year. In such a situation, the fall in capital shares could easily be 50% or more.

This is just not a risk worth taking. Some people argue that the past 28 years may be unrepresentative, because inflation was generally high, and we may now be in a low inflation era. There is some weight in this argument (if indeed it is true that inflation at high levels is over) as discussed under 'Positive indicators for capital shares' below. But I would not advise you to bet heavily against history, and anyone who buys capital shares when the market PE is high (as it is now) is doing just that.

➜ an update

My instincts were right. The markets were weak in 1994 and most capital shares fell, although somewhat less than might have been expected. The sector appears to have gone through a deserved re-rating.

Market vulnerability indicator (B): Yield

The market may be about to fall if the dividend yield is below 4%
Historically, dividend yields on the market as a whole have tended to be in the 4–6% range. BZW data on yields go back to 1918, and show that when the yield was below 4% (as when this book went to print), the average rise in the index was only 0.3%. With the ever onward march of the returns guaranteed to other classes of unit trust shareholders, this would almost certainly mean a substantial decline in the price of capital shares. Conversely, when the market yielded over 5%, the returns for the stock market over the next year averaged nearly 16%. This would generally mean a very healthy rise in capital share prices.

Market vulnerability indicator (C): Index Linked Gilt yield gap

The market may be about to fall if the stock market dividend yield falls below that on index linked gilts
From the mid-nineteenth to the mid-twentieth centuries, the normal expectation was that the yield on shares should be higher than that on gilts. The absence or reversal of this 'yield gap' (that is, whenever shares yielded the same as or less than gilts) was a reliable 'sell' indicator for shares.

Once Harold Macmillan ushered in the world of 'never had it so good', however, and inflation took off, the old relationship was obscured by inflation. Only in 1981, with the invention of Index Linked Gilts, was it possible to reconstruct a reliable new yield gap measure. Since 1981 the yield on shares has generally been above that on Index Linked Gilts. Only in 1987 did it fall below (and well below), giving a reliable (but generally ignored) signal to sell. To be safe, I would suggest that you avoid buying capital shares when the yield gap is only 0.5% or less (or negative). As this book went to press, the gap was down to about 0.5%.

Share prices like low inflation.

Positive indicators for capital shares

By way of contrast to the negative indicators above, there are two indicators which tend to be positive for the stock market as a whole and are highly relevant to the potential investor in SLIT capital shares.

Positive indicator A: Low inflation

One of the most neglected, but most interesting relationships is between stock market advances and low inflation. Because of the relevance of the relationship to all investment activity, however, it is worth more than a brief digression.

Share prices like low inflation. The evidence is overwhelming. As shown in Figure IX.8, the average real return on shares (i.e., the return after deducting inflation) since 1918 has been over 15% per annum when inflation has been below 2%, has been around 10–11% when inflation has been 2–6%, and has been very poor when inflation has been over 6% (and actually negative when inflation has been over 10%).

This table should be magnified and stuck up above the desk of every serious investor! Low inflation bumps up the prices of bonds and lowers their yield, which makes share yields look more attractive. There are two other reasons which are probably important in explaining the correlation between low inflation and high stock market advances. One is that in periods of low inflation, savers (including institutions) find it difficult to find any home for their savings in the bank or building society that appears to offer a reasonable rate of return, and so turn to the stock market. By contrast, when inflation is (say) 12% and interest rates are 15%, it looks much

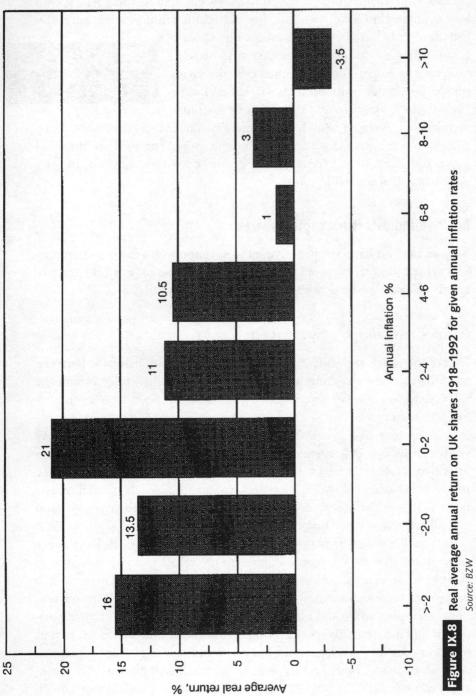

Figure IX.8 Real average annual return on UK shares 1918–1992 for given annual inflation rates
Source: BZW

safer and more attractive to lock in this return by a bank deposit than to chance one's arm in the stock market. The other explanation is that low inflation encourages long-term investment by industry, which is the only secure, long-term basis of wealth generation. But whatever the real reasons (and these cannot be proven statistically), the evidence over three quarters of a century is quite compelling. The best estimates for inflation over the next few years in the UK, as this book goes to press, are around the 3–5% mark. This is one reason why, despite the heights of the stock market in the second half of 1993 and the first half of 1994, I am optimistic about the *long-term* market prospects, once the inevitable short-term market setback has taken place.

From the viewpoint of the capital shareholder, however, what matters is not so much the *real* return on equities as the *nominal* return (including inflation), since the articles of SLITs are based on nominal returns for the other shareholders. And herein lies a curious paradox. You would imagine that the capital share investor would prefer high inflation to low inflation, since if inflation is (say) 10% or more, even a zero rate of real return would mean that most capital shares are undervalued today (as we saw in the three examples earlier, a 10% appreciation in the stock market each year would see an annual return to capital shareholders of between 14.8% and 49.2% and an average of virtually 30%). But

> ...... **No one set of data should determine your decision to buy such a risky instrument as SLIT capital shares.** ....

the rule, based on the BZW data from 1918 to 1992, seems to be that under high inflation the real returns can be negative, and nominal returns disappointing. Adding back the inflation rate, the returns are still greater when inflation is low than when it is high. As Figure IX.9 shows, when inflation is below 6%, the nominal increase in the stock market each year averages well over 10% (in fact, close to 16%), whereas above 6% inflation the average increase in the stock market tends to be 8–11%.

No one set of data should determine your decision to buy such a risky instrument as SLIT capital shares, but the least that can be said is that low inflation should give a clear positive indicator, and in the absence of any of the three negative indicators above, a degree of confidence for the long-term investor to buy.

> **→ an update**
>
> In 1996, Roger Bootle, the distinguished economist, wrote The Death of Inflation (publisher: Nicholas Brealey), suggesting that we are reverting to the pre-1945 world without perpetual inflation, where prices and wages will rise in some years but be static or fall in others; where house prices are as likely to fall as to rise; and where interest rates hover mainly in the 2–4% range.
>
> Bootle's evidence and logic impress me. If he is right, this could be very significant. Low inflation has nearly always been associated with a very positive long-term outlook for shares. If this relationship continues to hold, SLIT capital shares should do very well over the long haul.

Positive indicator B: Falling interest rates

Partly because of the correlation with low inflation, but mainly because bonds become less attractive and equities more, falling interest rates are generally good for equity markets. As far as I am aware, no statistical study has yet been undertaken of the effect of falling interest rates on the prices of SLIT capital shares, but it is pretty clear from observation that the effect tends to be highly positive.

Weighing up positive and negative indicators

> The effect of falling interest rates on the prices of SLIT capital shares . . . tends to be highly positive.

It is rare in real life that all the indicators line up the way you would want them, so judgment has to be exercised. For the short-term investor, I would suggest that at least one of the two positive indicators should exist, plus (most importantly) none of the negative indicators. If you are a long-term investor, prepared and able to take some risks, you *might* decide to invest given two positive indicators and the existence of only one of the three negative indicators. But neither the short- nor the long-term investor should put more than a maximum of 25% of their portfolio at any one time into SLIT capital shares, and 10–20% would be a more comfortable amount.

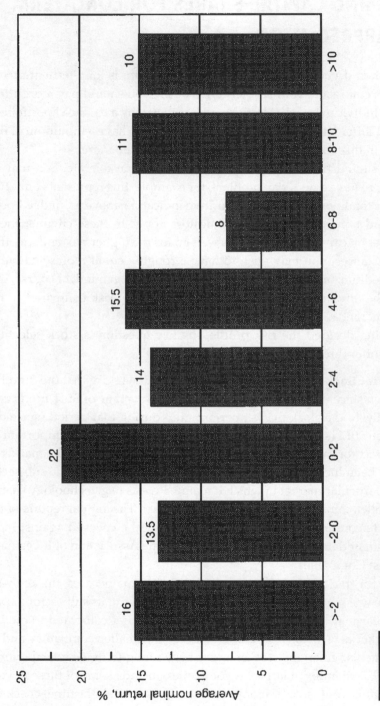

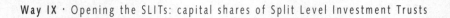

Figure IX.9 Nominal average annual return on UK shares 1918–1992 for give annual inflation rates

Source: BZW

USING CAPITAL SHARES FOR LONG-TERM APPRECIATION

How should you select capital shares if your aim is long-term appreciation? In contrast to your shorter-term cousin, you should pay more attention to individual stock selection and less to having a balanced portfolio of several different shares. It is probably still wise to have a minimum of five shares in this part of your portfolio, but perhaps no more.

You should first decide the risk profile you can tolerate. You may be willing to have a high risk profile if, for example, this represents only 10% of your total portfolio, the two positive indicators above are indeed positive, and none of the negative indicators apply. In these circumstances, your bet on capital shares may as well go for the higher risk end. In other circumstances, you may wish to have a roughly equal representative of low, medium and high risk capital shares (bearing in mind, of course, that even the 'low' risk ones represent above average risk compared to the stock market as a whole).

Having decided the risk profile, the key question is stock selection. Here I offer three guidelines:

1. **Go for track record of the fund.** Calculate the return that the fund has given since its inception. Compare it to the average of SLIT funds generally, to the stock market performance during that period (since different SLITs have been set up at different times it is important to correct for this to see whether the SLIT really has beaten the market or just been lucky in the time it started), and if possible to the sub-sector or particular market in which it mainly invests (e.g. technology shares, smaller companies, emerging markets, etc.). The annual reports of the SLITs concerned will help here, but should be checked against independent data, such as that published by the Association of Investment Trust Companies.

2. **Go for track record of the market sector.** In many cases, the key variable will not be the fund's performance relative to its sub-sector or particular market, but the performance of the latter compared to the UK market as a whole. As mentioned above, smaller companies and in particular emerging stock markets have a long-term record superior to the FT-SE index of large UK companies. Include some of these in your portfolio, but (since sector performance changes all the time) check the

most recent data in as disaggregated fashion as possible before making your investment.

3. **Go for capital share value.** Based on (1) and (2) above, and on the valuation techniques discussed earlier in this chapter, construct your own scenario for the expected value of a long list of possible SLIT capital shares (for example, if you want to invest in five, look at a list of 10–15 possible candidates which appear to satisfy conditions (1) and (2) over the time period you have for investment). Select the shares which appear to offer the best gross redemption yield characteristics, after checking that the risk is acceptable. You might want to do this separately for your low-, medium- and high-risk candidates, because otherwise you could end up selecting just high-risk shares (these will naturally tend to have the highest expected value yields).

✔ Advantages...   *of SLIT capital shares*

1. They are a geared instrument offering high potential returns, especially when (either over the short or long term) stock markets are rising. After the requirements of the other shareholders have been met, the capital shareholders scoop all the excess profits available. A relatively small increase in the rate of annual returns to the fund as a whole can lead to large increases in returns to the capital shareholders.

2. Relative to other geared instruments such as options (or even warrants, the subject of the next chapter), SLIT capital shares have low spreads, high liquidity and generally long terms to maturity. These characteristics make them better value and actually lower risk than most instruments with comparable upside.

3. It is possible to lower (although not eliminate) the risk involved, by looking carefully at history and current market conditions before investing.

4. They are under-researched and under-invested by institutions. This means that market anomalies occur that can be picked out and benefited from by the private investor.

5. Notwithstanding point (4), the degree of research, knowledge and acceptance of these shares is increasing. As more institutions move into them, the high current discounts to net asset value may narrow significantly. There are grounds for thinking that SLIT capital shares as a whole are seriously undervalued, and this may be less true in the future.

6. The underlying investment focus of many SLITs (especially in international markets, fast-growth stock markets and smaller companies) may well lead them to out-perform the normal UK market indices.

7. Profits come in the form of capital gains, which can lead to the deferment or, in some cases, avoidance of taxation, depending on investors' personal tax circumstances.

✗ Disadvantages... *of SLIT capital shares*

1. They are inherently risky and this risk can never be eliminated. They stand at the back of the queue of creditors for payment when the trust is wound up. They should not comprise a total portfolio on their own.

2. Calculating their value is difficult and controversial. They are only suitable for sophisticated and number-loving investors.

3. In the short term, their values can crash alarmingly if the market as a whole declines.

4. In the long term, they may become worthless. If the market as a whole fails to advance year by year, a portfolio of capital shares may not diversify away much or any of the risk.

5. They do not pay dividends.

WHO ARE THESE SHARES FOR?

These are shares for analysts par excellence. Along with warrants (coming next!) they are a trap for those who do not like complicated calculations! They also require the ability to be dispassionate about the evidence and act accordingly. They should be avoided by those who are prone to over-optimism.

These shares are also for the well-heeled. Arguably, anyone can put a portion of their portfolio (perhaps up to 10%) into these shares, but they must be willing to lose it! Even the rich are advised to restrict the proportion of these shares in their portfolio to a maximum of 25% of the total value, unless the value has already increased enormously!

▶ Overall evaluation

SLIT capital shares are clearly risky, but in my opinion can offer an excellent risk-reward relationship. The most important thing with these shares is timing, and this relates much more to overall market conditions than to the differential prospects of particular shares. If the timing is right, or the shares are bought little by little over a long period, the returns could be spectacular … or nil!

Warrants

This Way is for well-heeled, analytical investors who can afford to take risks with part of their portfolio.

For sophisticates and risk takers only!

What are warrants?

Which shares have warrants?

A list of chunky warrants

Investment in warrants: when and which?

Why do warrants favour individuals over institutions?

Who is this Way best for?

Overall evaluation

FOR SOPHISTICATES AND RISK TAKERS ONLY!

Warrants are a fast growing and fascinating investment medium. If used properly they offer much better value and are a lower risk than more well-known speculative media such as traditional options, traded options and 'index' bets on stock market direction. There are, however, *two big 'Buts'* surrounding warrants:

- Warrants should not be viewed as an accessible 'punt' for the average investor: they are far too dangerous for this. Warrants should only be invested in by those who are financially sophisticated and highly numerate.

- Even then, warrants are the highest risk approach to investment recommended in this book. This chapter is therefore only for those who can really afford to take chances with their money. This Way should not be used by anyone as their sole investment approach. Even if you are a risk taker, do not put more than 20% of your investment funds into warrants.

WHAT ARE WARRANTS?

A warrant is a right to buy shares in a company at a particular price at specified future dates. The conversion price may be higher than the current stock market price of the shares, but since the warrant is a lot cheaper than the shares you can buy more warrants, and thus the right to more shares in the future, than you could if you just bought the shares instead. The warrant is itself traded on the stock exchange. It is rather like a long-term traded option.

There are therefore two ways to make money out of warrants:

1. by waiting until the share price goes up (and the time for conversion arrives), and then converting the warrants into shares, **or**
2. by selling when the warrant goes up in value (this will normally happen when the shares in the relevant company go up, even if the conversion time ('exercise period') is still well in the future).

Warrants therefore offer the potential for high capital gains (warrants do not pay dividends) when shares go up, and have the corresponding downside of rapid loss of value when shares go down. In general, warrants will go up faster than shares in bull markets and fall faster in bear markets.

> ......In general, warrants will go up faster than shares in bull markets and fall faster in bear markets. ....

Warrants are therefore 'geared' investments, and riskier than buying shares. They are, however, safer than buying options, because the time period for the underlying shares to appreciate is so much longer. They are also generally better value than options, because the transactions cost element is lower.

There are a number of ways in which the risk of buying warrants can be reduced. Warrants are especially interesting for the private investor who does his own calculations, because this is an under-researched area where the private investor can have structural advantages over the institutions.

To illustrate how warrants work, I have constructed a hypothetical example of a mythical company.

Upwardly Mobile Plc

✳ EXAMPLE Upwardly Mobile Plc (UMP) is one of the companies that has warrants as well as ordinary shares. The shares are priced at 100p. Each warrant allows you to buy one share in UMP on or before 1 January 1995 at a conversion price also of 100p (this is a convenience to make calculations easier). The warrants trade on the stock market for 20p.

Helen and Rupert are both wealthy and sophisticated private investors. They are also friends who swap notes on their investments. They have both conducted fundamental analysis which leads them to be very positive about UMP shares, which are demonstrating accelerated earnings but still only trade on a modest rating. They both decide to allocate £20,000 to UMP.

Rupert does the obvious thing and buys 20,000 UMP shares. Helen is more adventurous and buys the warrants instead, obtaining 100,000 UMP warrants.

They are right about UPM's prospects. By the end of 1994 UMP has reported a surge in earnings and the shares gallop ahead to 150p, producing a 50% hike for Rupert. But the warrants have gone up to 70p, producing a 250% gain for Helen.

Why does this happen? We assume, in this simplified example, that there is a 20p 'premium' throughout in the warrants, over and above the conversion (or 'intrinsic') value of the warrants into shares. The 'premium' is for the benefits the warrants confer, mainly the gearing effect itself. When Helen bought the warrants, the 'intrinsic' value of the warrants was nil, because UMP shares were 100p and the right to convert was also at 100p. The 20p Helen paid was all 'premium' value.

But when Helen came to sell the warrants, the UMP shares had gone to 150p and therefore each warrant had an intrinsic value of 50p (she could have converted the warrants into shares worth 150p by only paying 100p). This 50p plus the premium of 20p explains why she could sell the warrants at 70p.

But why would the premium still be worth paying? If the shares went from 150p to 200p, the 'intrinsic' value would rise to 100p (200p minus 100p), and even without any premium value remaining, the warrants would therefore go up 43% (from 70p to 100p), significantly more than the 33% advance in the share price. (If the premium value remained at 20p, the warrants would now be worth 120p, a rise of 71%. The premium would disappear, however, when the warrants reached the end of their conversion period.)

What if Helen and Rupert had been wrong about UMP?

The catch with warrants, of course, is what would have happened if they had been wrong, and UMP's earnings growth had gone into reverse. What if the shares fell from 100p to 50p?

Rupert's loss is easy to calculate: 50%. For Helen, our mechanistic example would suggest that the warrants become worthless, because the 20p of premium value would be more than wiped out by the minus 50p of intrinsic value. But this would be wrong, since there is no obligation on the part of warrant holders to convert, and they would not do so. The intrinsic value would remain at zero, but what would happen is that the premium value would fall dramatically, because very few investors would believe that UMP shares would ever be worth more than 100p. In these circumstances the warrants might fall to, say, 5p, causing Helen a loss of 75%.

Alternatively, assume that Helen and Rupert were right in the short term and did manage to sell their warrants (at 70p) and shares (at 150p) respectively, and that they were bought by Fiona and Simon respectively, but that the shares then fell back to 100p. Simon would suffer a 33% loss on his shares, but the price of the warrants would fall from 70p back to 20p, causing Fiona a 71% loss.

If you have followed this example, you should already have a good intuitive feel for how warrants work. Before getting more technical (which, alas, we shall have to do) let me interest you with a real example.[1]

✳ EXAMPLE   **Airtours**

During the first ten months of 1991 the shares of Airtours, the package holiday operators, rose from 170p to 812p – a very impressive 378% gain! Rupert, or his functional equivalent, would have been very pleased. But it so happens that Airtours is of one the companies that has warrants, which Helen could have bought at the start of 1991 for 12p (that includes the jobber's spread: the middle market price was 10p). By the end of October 1991, the warrants had ascended to 590p, a rise of 4,817%!

If Rupert and Helen had both invested £10,000, Rupert's profit on the shares would have been a handsome £37,800, but Helen's bonanza on the warrants would have been £481,700! It should be added that in practice Helen would have found it difficult to buy that many warrants without driving the price up, but it does illustrate the value of gearing provided by warrants.

▌ WHICH SHARES HAVE WARRANTS?

Sadly, though warrants are the fastest growing sector of the UK stock market, it is only a minority of companies that have issued warrants. There are some 200 or so warrants listed on the stock exchange, of which one-third belong to normal commercial companies and two-thirds to investment

---

* I am indebted both for this example and for much more to Andrew McHattie, whose companion book, *The Investors's Guide to Warrants* (also published by Financial Times/Pitman Publishing) is indispensable for the serious investor in warrants.

trusts. The growth of warrants has been driven by new issues of investment trusts. Both categories are interesting media for investment.

Yet, for the serious investor wishing to make substantial and liquid investments, there are regrettably not 200-plus warrants in which to invest. Many of the warrants listed have very low market capitalisations and are difficult and expensive to deal in. We therefore need to narrow the field down to a smaller number of 'quality' warrants that are of interest to the serious investor. These I call 'chunky' warrants.

A LIST OF CHUNKY WARRANTS

How 'chunky' a warrants needs to be depends on the quantities that you wish to buy, or, more precisely, your average size of investment. If you are happy to invest in lots of £1,000 or £2,000, then you may regard all 200-odd warrants as being chunky enough for your requirements. (You will pay quite substantial transactions costs, though.) But if you have a minimum investment rule of £5,000, quite a few of the warrants will rule themselves out, as you may find it difficult to buy, and even more difficult to sell, without moving the price.

At the other extreme, there are a few warrants capitalised at over £100m in which even large investors can deal. 'Chunkiness' is therefore a subjective criterion. I have adopted two stringent criteria, to give a list of the most chunky warrants. To be included on my list, warrants must (1) be quoted in the *Financial Times* daily, and (2) have a minimum market value of £5m. At £5m, a £10,000 investment comprises 0.2% of the shares, and therefore should not move the price, particularly as there can be arbitrage between the warrants and the underlying shares, which will always have a much higher market value.

The list given below is of all warrants that satisfied the criteria as at 11 September 1993 and is 'directional' as warrant values can change quickly. There are 26 in total, of which only 9 (printed in bold below) are in commercial companies (the rest are in investment trusts). Since 5 of the 9 are warrants in the same company (BTR), the choice of really chunky commercial warrants quoted in the *FT* is restricted to BTR, Eurotunnel, Hanson, Lucas, and Yorkshire-TyneTees TV.

Table X.1   'Chunky' Warrants as at 11 September 1993

Rank	Warrant	Market value (£m)
1	**BTR 94/95**	**288.2**
2	**BTR 97**	**153.9**
3	**BTR 95/96**	**150.6**
4	**BTR 92/93**	**128.1**
5	**Eurotunnel**	**114.8**
6	**BTR 93/94**	**78.5**
7	**Hanson**	**44.8**
8	Scottish Investment Trust	34.8
9	Fleming Japan Investment Trust	25.4
10	Foreign & Colonial Pacific Investment Trust	19.9
11	Templeton Emerging Markets Investment Trust	16.6
12	**Lucas Industries**	**13.7**
13	Latin American Investment Trust	12.1
14	European Smaller Companies Investment Trust	11.6
15	English & Scottish Investment Trust	10.7
16	Aberforth Smaller Companies Investment Trust	10.0
17	Fleming Emerging Markets Investment Trust	9.2
18	Fidelity European Values Investment Trust	7.6
19	Gartmore Emerging Pacific Investment Trust	7.3
20	Beta Global Emerging Markets Investment Trust	6.8
21	Perpetual Japan Investment Trust	6.7
22	Abtrust New Dawn Investment Trust	6.5
23	US Smaller Companies Investment Trust	6.3
24	Moorgate Smaller Companies Investment Trust	5.5
25	**Yorkshire-Tyne Tees TV**	**5.0**
26	Foreign & Colonial US Smaller Companies Investment Trust	5.0

INVESTMENT IN WARRANTS: WHEN AND WHICH?

There should be three stages to consider, in sequence, when considering investment in warrants. You should only invest when you have positive answers to all three. They are:

1. Market direction
2. Fundamental analysis
3. Technical analysis

1. Market direction

Remember that in large part warrants are a bet that the stock market is headed upward. For the long-term investor this is probably a good bet, but in the short term the warrant buyer could lose most or all of the investment if the market heads south.

In general, therefore, you should not buy warrants if the stock market is currently moving sideways or down, however attractive the company in whose warrants you wish to invest. There will probably be opportunities to buy the warrants at cheaper prices later. A guide to the extent of market vulnerability has been given in the previous chapter (see pages 255–261) and should be reviewed prior to investing in warrants.

2. Fundamental analysis

You should not buy warrants unless you would, in the absence of warrants existing, buy the shares of the company involved. This means that you must have some rational basis for wanting an investment in the company concerned. You must therefore determine your attitude to the companies which have warrants. For the serious investor wanting 'chunky' industrial/commercial (as opposed to investment trust) warrants, therefore, you must determine your attitude towards BTR, Eurotunnel, Hanson and Lucas. Hanson and BTR are conglomerates with excellent long-term track records, although conglomerates are currently out of fashion and the opportunities for old-fashioned hostile bids appear limited. Eurotunnel is perhaps an analyst's dream share, in that it is highly geared operationally, and opinions differ hugely on future cashflows, with the result that the shares have been and will be very volatile. Be aware that to buy Eurotunnel warrants is to make a bet with large upside and downside. Lucas's volatility is less than Eurotunnel, but still above average. You should not invest in any of these warrants without conducting your own fundamental analysis of their shares' (or companies') prospects.

It is, however, quite possible for the warrant investor to ignore the few large industrial companies that have warrants and concentrate instead on investment trusts. These will tend to follow the direction of the market as a whole, but different investment trusts have different investment foci and philosophies, and it is important to understand these. The investment trust warrant buyer must therefore look at each trust's investment focus and approach, and its track record, before deciding which if any to invest in.

The investment focus will be spelt out clearly in the marketing literature and annual reports of the trust concerned. A few of the trusts listed above as having 'chunky' warrants are general investment trusts, but most have a geographical focus, or a focus on smaller companies, or both.

About half of the trusts have a focus on 'emerging' markets, that is, markets with high GDP growth but underdeveloped stock markets, especially in Latin America, the Far East and Eastern Europe. Some confine themselves to particular regions but most do not. There are currently several very good reasons for investment in emerging markets, and these are listed in Way VIII. You should read this chapter carefully to see whether you agree with the reasons given, and to look at the risks involved. Remember also that although the recent track record of most emerging market trusts is very good, this trend could easily go into reverse, and the risks for warrant holders are greatly magnified even relative to the high risk borne by buyers of shares in these investment trusts.

Trusts that have a geographic focus on developed markets generally focus on Europe, America or Japan. Before buying warrants in these trusts you must have good reason for thinking that these stock markets will appreciate, and that sterling will not against the dollar or yen. You should also check that dollar or yen are not vulnerable to a fall in their exchange rate against the pound.

Smaller company investment trusts also display greater volatility than those that invest in mature companies. It is generally a mistake to buy a geared investment in smaller companies when the economy is moving into, or stuck in, a recession, as small companies are more vulnerable then.

On top of the markets selected, you should evaluate the investment trust for its record *in its chosen field, relative to other comparable investment trusts*. Although, as they say, past performance is no guarantee of future performance, my preference is always to back winners rather than losers within a carefully segmented category.

3. Technical analysis

Most that is written on warrants tends to focus on how good value the warrants are, relative to other warrants: this is the domain of technical analysis. This is clearly very important, but in many ways it is less important than whether a leveraged investment in the company concerned is advisable. An exclusive focus on the technical side of warrants is similar to the racecourse punter who wants to get a better price from the bookmakers than the starting price, without worrying about the form of the horses and which one is likely to win. It is better to buy a bad value warrant in a company that is headed north than to

> Smaller company investment trusts display greater volatility than those that invest in mature companies.

buy an excellent value warrant in a company whose share price is about to fall. The serious investor in warrants will master the technical factors, but will never forget that points (1) and (2) above are essential to evaluate first.

It is beyond the scope of this chapter to give any more than a rudimentary guide to the technical side of warrants, which should be followed up by reading Andrew McHattie's book, *The Investor's Guide to Warrants*, referred to earlier.

(a) Price premium

In the earlier example of Upwardly Mobile plc, the principle of the conversion price premium was explained. The formula for the premium is as follows:

$$\text{Premium (\%)} = \frac{\text{Warrant price + Exercise price - Share price}}{\text{Share price}} \times 100$$

In the case of Upwardly Mobile plc, this calculation is:

$$\text{Premium on UMP warrants} = \frac{20p = 100p - 100p}{100p} \times 100 = 20\%$$

The lower the premium, the better value the warrants technically.

(b) Time to expiry

The premium is of only limited relevance without considering also the time period within which the warrant is allowed to be exercised (that is, converted into ordinary shares). A very low premium would not be interesting if the warrants were about to expire, whereas a very high premium might be good value if the warrants could be exercised at any time up to the year 2050!

On average, warrants have four to five years to go before maturity (final expiry), but this is only an average and there is considerable variation. The risk is clearly much greater with a short time to expiry, and unless you are confident that the shares will appreciate in the short term you should steer clear of warrants with, say, less than two years to run.

(c) The capital fulcrum point

For experts on warrants, the capital fulcrum point (CFP) is the key ratio to consider. For non-experts, or those with only rusty algebra, the formula is frightening. Let me try to explain it in words.

The CFP really tries to answer the question: Will I be better off buying the shares of a company, or its warrants? In general, if you expect high appreciation of the shares, it will be better to buy the warrants. But at what point does it become better?

The answer is: at the CFP! A growth rate in share value above the CFP is a signal to buy the warrants, at below the CFP, not to (that is, buy the shares or nothing, but not the warrants). Assume that you believe that Upwardly Mobile plc shares will appreciate on average by 12% per annum, and the CFP is 10%, then you should buy the warrants rather than the shares. If you thought the shares would go up by 9%, and this was above your investment target, you would be better off buying the shares than the warrants.

Assume that someone else calculates the CFP for you. As a general rule, a CFP above 10 will mean that the warrants are poor value relative to the underlying shares. Conversely, a CFP of 6 to 8 (or lower) can mean that the warrants with a long time to expiry are good value, even if the premium is high. The CFP is a better guide to underlying value than the premium alone.

People who want to become experts at warrants will have plenty of time to learn how to calculate the CFP for themselves, as well as to wallow in other formulae of a type to fascinate those with A Level or degree expertise in mathematics and computing. All this lies well beyond my own expertise, so I will move on to summarise the attractions and dangers of investment in warrants.

WHY DO WARRANTS FAVOUR INDIVIDUALS OVER INSTITUTIONS?

Warrants are particularly interesting for the intelligent private investor who is prepared to spend time and effort analysing them. There are five reasons why:

1. Size of investment

Warrants are almost unique in having their fundamental value determined by large liquidity instruments (the shares in companies that also have warrants) but by being low liquidity instruments themselves. This means that the spreads on warrants are not ruinously large – as with 'penny shares' – but that most warrants are of little or no interest to institutions, simply because the market capitalisations are not large enough. Remember that most institutions are not interested in investing in instruments with a total value of less than £25m, and (in September 1993) only nine warrants in Table X.1 on page 274 passed this test. For most warrants, therefore, institutions cannot buy in or sell in the quantities they would like, which leaves the field open for the smart private investor to go for value when it appears.

> For most warrants, institutions cannot buy in or sell in the quantities they would like.

2. Market imperfections abound

The warrants market is under-researched, mainly because the institutions (the effective market for most research) have little interest. This means that the keen amateur can spot bargains well ahead even of the market makers.

3. Private investors matter

Those brokers who deal in warrants are aware that their bread and butter comes from private investors. They will not, therefore, be treated as second-class citizens after the institutions.

4. The warrants market is growing

Increasingly, the rate of new warrants issues is faster than the retirement rate of existing warrants. It is also likely that the market in 'chunky' warrants will grow. This gives advantages to the private investor used to evaluating warrants, when they will be competing with institutions.

5. It is likely that more institutions will enter the warrants market

As the number of warrants in issue, the average market capitalisation, and knowledge about warrants all grow, it is increasingly likely that institutions will enter the market for buying warrants. This is likely to increase the premiums paid for warrants, and move the whole warrants market up.

✔ Advantages... *of warrants*

1. As we have seen, the gearing effect of warrants can produce large gains when the underlying shares move up. Effectively warrants offer the possibility of buying into a larger number of shares for the same amount of money, which explains how Helen was able to make more money than Rupert out of Upwardly Mobile plc.
2. Warrants are under-researched and offer the private investor the advantages enumerated above.
3. An investor who buys a portfolio of warrants, cuts his or her losses on those that go down, and plays those that go up for a longer period of time, can emerge with an excellent average return even if the majority of the warrants in the portfolio decline.
4. Warrants that have a long time to expiry are much less speculative and subject to short-term market corrections than options or other derivative instruments.
5. Most warrants are in investment trusts with an orientation to smaller

companies or international markets. These have demonstrated above average capital growth in the past and are likely to do so again in the future. The warrants are a leveraged instrument in trusts which, while not being unduly speculative themselves, are likely to demonstrate above average performance. This combination of a geared return in what should be a good and reasonably conservative long-term bet is an unusually attractive proposition.

✗ Disadvantages... *of warrants*

1. The first disadvantage is the reverse of the first advantage: the gearing effect can magnify losses as well as gains. If you buy warrants, keep repeating to yourself as you go: I could lose all this money. If the share price falls below the exercise price and stays there, the warrant will be worthless.
2. Warrants are more expensive to buy and sell than shares, in that the spreads are greater.
3. Liquidity is much poorer for most warrants than most shares. The difficulty is greatest with the less 'chunky' warrants. This may make it difficult to buy the quantity you want without paying over the odds, and even more difficult to sell when you want or need to, without taking a bath.
4. Warrants do not pay any dividends, and so are unsuitable for those who want income. Nor do they give you any voting rights or access to shareholders' meetings (though those who have had this privilege may count its absence a benefit).
5. Warrants are only available in an infuriatingly restricted list of companies, and as shown above, in only about 25 to any reasonable degree of liquidity.

WHO IS THIS WAY BEST FOR?

The answer is clear: the rich, the risk taker, the sophisticated, the analyst, the time-rich, the algebraic, the quant-jock, the visionary, the patient, the opinionated, and, above all, the private investor. Preferably, all of the above!

But let us repeat: do not put more than 20% of your portfolio in war-

Do not put more than 20% of your portfolio in warrants, even if you have an identikit match with the profile above.

rants, even if you have an identikit match with the profile above. This is not an approach for widows, orphans or office workers.

➤ Overall evaluation

This approach offers financial engineering in basically sound companies: the most conservative form of extreme speculation known to mankind. It is really only for the most expert of private investors, but I cannot think of a better reason for the hard work involved in becoming an expert. As such, warrants are a worthy close to this book.

Conclusion

Ten ways to compound wealth

None of the Ways recommended is a licence for the lazy to get rich quick. All of the Ways are encouragement to the industrious and creative elements in our society to apply the same mixture of effort and inspiration to the compounding of wealth as to its original creation.

Becoming an expert in investment means focusing on an approach which is compatible with your personality and maximises the spin-offs from

> **Beating the market is both possible and fun.**

your normal work and leisure pursuits ... and working hard at it. The magic of compounding wealth means it is worth the effort. Beating the market is both possible and fun. If you fail: cut your losses. Hand your money management over to others and enjoy the rest of life. If you succeed, to a small degree as a result of this book, do something worthwhile with at least some of your wealth.

Index